THE

ONE LIGHT AHEAD

UNDATED 16-MONTH SELF-LEADERSHIP PLANNER

Prepare and Intentionally Create Lightbulb Moments Every Day

BELONGS TO

_____

_____

©April Ballestero

www.onelightacademy.net; coachapril@onelightacademy.net

www.kaleidoscopebooks.net

Kaleidoscope Publishing

The One Light Ahead Undated 16-Month Self-Leadership Planner: Prepare and Intentionally Create Lightbulb Moments Every Day by April Ballestero
Copyright © 2023 April Ballestero

ISBN: 979-8-9893127-0-2

This title and *Slaying the Onion: Unveil the Layers of Your Story to Reveal Your Highest Potential* available at www.kaleidoscopebooks.net

Requests for information should be addressed to: Kaleidoscope Publishing, 1738 Oak Trail St. NE, Massillon, OH 44646

Cover graphic: Stephanie Arnold

For more information about the author visit www.onelightacademy.net

Dear friend,

Thank you for investing in yourself!

You might be wondering how a planner can help with personal self-leadership. You've probably noticed habits and patterns, beliefs, and personal challenges you'd like to change or overcome. I call those *opportunities*. We are so prone to filling our schedule with a To Do List. Tasks that need to be done for our lives, our family, our company, or our job. Yet, too often, we neglect becoming and *being* our best selves.

This planner is a very personal product for me. It's about taking steps toward becoming and *being*. It's about facing the many layers inside us with honesty and personal integrity.

In my decades of serving as a business and life coach, I have learned that leading by example is one of the best gifts I can give a client. That's not to say I'm perfect in any way. Rather, my greatest joy is often found in coming alongside others on life's journey. So here I am, sharing with **you** the techniques I use for myself and what I teach others, as we pursue reaching our highest potential.

The guides contained in this planner can provide us with visual reference points regarding our goals and measurable action steps to execute on a daily, weekly, and monthly basis. By using the Life Wheel for monthly self-assessment and completing the reflection exercises, we can see if what we *say* matters to us truly matters. Are we consistent in how we make choices? Are our commitments supporting what is most important to us?

Seeing where we are creates the opportunity for light bulb moments, insight, and revelation we can immediately use to our advantage. Then we can make real choices—choices that may take us where we want to go and help us be who we want to be.

These pages provide an amazing opportunity to reflect on every aspect of our lives. Successes we achieve and goals for the future. Remember, you're not alone. I'll be doing the same exercises and self-reflection to create and track improvement. Finding personal and professional balance isn't easy, yet with daily intentionality we can make progress.

Find my Facebook group at https://www.facebook.com/SlayingtheOnion or find me at coachapril@onelightacademy.net.

Looking forward to celebrating with you,

April

P.S. The Life Wheel exercise and quotes on the following pages come from my book *Slaying the Onion: Unveil the Layers of Your Story to Reach Your Highest Potential*. You can find it at www.kaleidoscopebooks.net or from any major retailer in paperback, eBook, and audiobook form.

P.P.S. If you really want to take it to the next level, please consider this your personal invite to take a FREE thought assessment that takes less than fifteen minutes at www.vqprofile.com/onelightahead and check out other resources at www.onelightacademy.org.

PERSONAL INFORMATION

Name: _____

Address: _____

Telephone: _____ Email: _____

Employer/Business: _____

Address: _____

Telephone: _____ Email: _____

MEDICAL INFORMATION

Physician: _____ Telephone: _____

Allergies: _____

Medications: _____

Blood Type: _____

Insurer: _____

Health Conditions of Note: _____

IN CASE OF EMERGENCY, NOTIFY

Name: _____

Address: _____

Telephone: _____ Relationship: _____

NOTES:

_____
_____
_____
_____
_____
_____
_____

NOTES

How to Use This Planner and Improve Your Life

Every day presents us with the same opportunity to be who we want to be. In every interaction with others and every moment to ourselves, we either take steps toward or steps away from that **reality**. Our lives consist of the **choices** we make and the circumstances we find ourselves in because of those choices.

Many people don't realize how often we all make choices. Habits, procedures, and practices can become such automatic responses we aren't really living. Yes, time is passing and tasks are being accomplished, yet the satisfaction our soul craves eludes us. At the end of today we lack fulfillment, which can lead to tomorrow's lack of motivation. For decades, I've helped my clients recognize how our choices produce short-term and long-term results, and how we can be more **present** in our own lives.

Here's the great news—we all hold the keys to our own freedom. Freedom from monotony, burnout, constant striving, people pleasing, or even imposter syndrome. When we're willing to **look in the mirror** and be honest with ourselves, we open the door to new possibilities. We can make choices that change our lives for the better by asking ourselves the central question: In this moment, what choice can I make and what action can I take to create the greatest net value?

In my book *Slaying the Onion*, I talk about how we all have many layers to our lives and ourselves. And we live in and are influenced by two worlds: our **external world** and our **internal world**. Our external world includes all that happens outside us. In other words, what can be seen and touched and sensed. Our internal world involves our mind, emotions, and soul or spirit. There's a lot going on in these worlds.

Those of us who seek to **Live Unlayered**—who want and work to live as our most authentic selves in both worlds, free of burdens, wounds, beliefs, and messages that don't serve us—are **Onion Slayers**. We face our true condition, then target and address the aspects we have the power to change, layer by layer by layer.

To see and track progress, we start by taking a baseline. The **Life Wheel** exercise offers **awareness** of our current level of satisfaction in various areas of our life. Feel free to change or add an area. If it's important to you, it's important.

On a scale of one to ten, one being the lowest of the low and ten being best, rate your level of fulfillment in each category and record on the Life Wheel.

Business Calling _____   Financial Health _____

Physical Wellness _____   Relational Health _____

Intimacy _____   Personal Development _____

Play Time/Fun _____   Spiritual Wellness _____

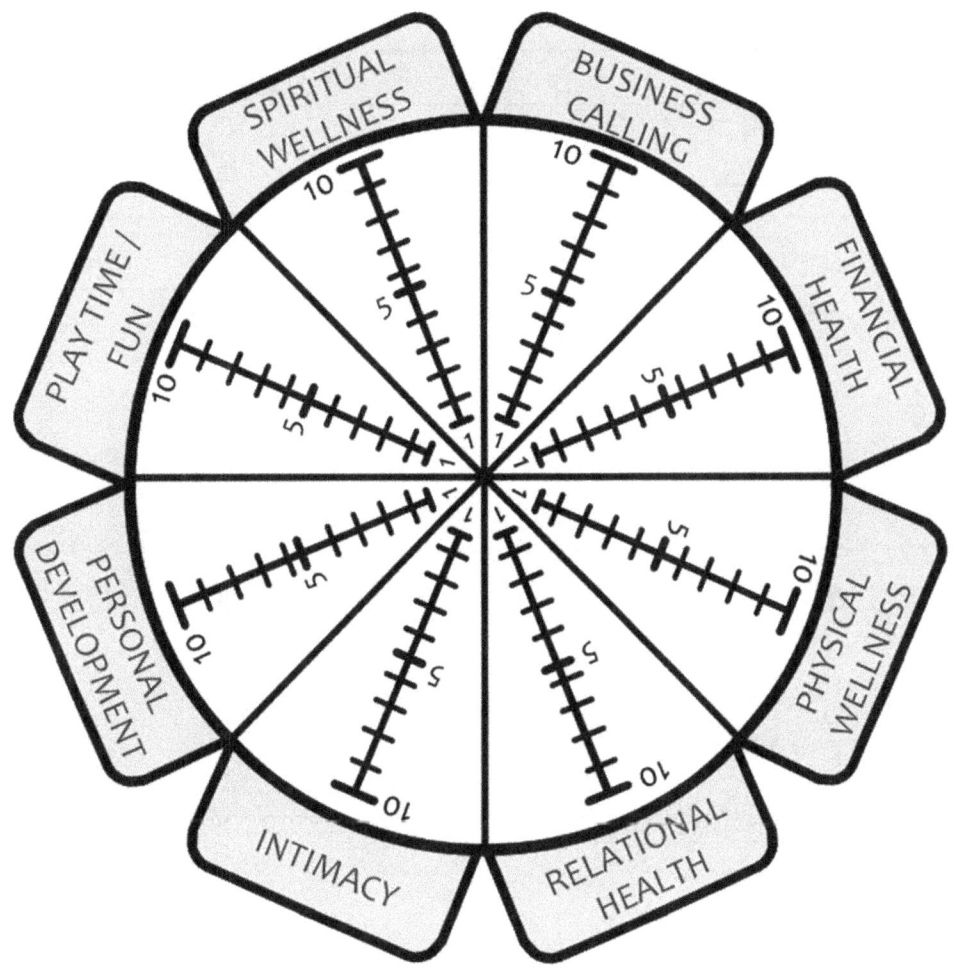

Now, connect your dots or marks. This might create a circle, a trapezoid, or some other figure you may not even know how to describe. Don't worry, that happens a lot. My point here to consider is this: If the wheels on the vehicle of your life that you drive every day are all *that shape*…how's the drive? A tad bumpy? Are you able to move in the direction you desire, at all?

Because awareness and **intentionality** are key to improvement in our personal and professional lives, we offer the Life Wheel exercise prior to every month. The information you glean from this tool can help you choose which areas are on your **radar**. Once you choose where to focus your efforts, you can determine and record viable **action steps** on your month overviews. And I strongly encourage you to update and change them as needed in your week overviews.

Finally, to track progress, we offer a self-reflection exercise after each month. Celebrating wins and being honest about challenges are necessary for **self-leadership** and when leading others. Be faithful to yourself and fully utilize all the features of this planner. And remember to join our Facebook group at https://tinyurl.com/3wfscxyn to receive ongoing encouragement. We are all on the same journey, learning to live unlayered.

Life Wheel Focus Area: *Business Calling: External Perspective*
What about this area is important to me?

_____

_____

MONTH: _____   YEAR: _____

Action Steps

_____

_____

_____

_____

_____

_____

_____

_____

_____

OPPORTUNITIES

- ☐ _____
- ☐ _____
- ☐ _____
- ☐ _____
- ☐ _____
- ☐ _____
- ☐ _____
- ☐ _____
- ☐ _____
- ☐ _____

SUNDAY	MONDAY	TUESDAY

NOTES:

Focus Verse: "A voice of one calling: 'In the wilderness prepare the way for the LORD; make straight in the desert a highway for our God.'" Isaiah 40:3

How does this verse apply to my external world?

_____

WEDNESDAY	THURSDAY	FRIDAY	SATURDAY

"Freedom facilitates freedom." p.9

WEEK OF _____ TO _____

Areas of my Life Wheel on my radar

_____

_____

_____

_____

MONDAY	TUESDAY	WEDNESDAY
5AM_____	5AM_____	5AM_____
_____	_____	_____
6AM_____	6AM_____	6AM_____
_____	_____	_____
7AM_____	7AM_____	7AM_____
_____	_____	_____
8AM_____	8AM_____	8AM_____
_____	_____	_____
9AM_____	9AM_____	9AM_____
_____	_____	_____
10AM_____	10AM_____	10AM_____
_____	_____	_____
11AM_____	11AM_____	11AM_____
_____	_____	_____
12PM_____	12PM_____	12PM_____
_____	_____	_____
1PM_____	1PM_____	1PM_____
_____	_____	_____
2PM_____	2PM_____	2PM_____
_____	_____	_____
3PM_____	3PM_____	3PM_____
_____	_____	_____
4PM_____	4PM_____	4PM_____
_____	_____	_____
5PM_____	5PM_____	5PM_____
_____	_____	_____
6PM_____	6PM_____	6PM_____
_____	_____	_____
7PM_____	7PM_____	7PM_____
_____	_____	_____
8PM_____	8PM_____	8PM_____
_____	_____	_____

SUNDAY

9AM_____
_____
10AM_____
_____
11AM_____
_____
12PM_____
_____
1PM_____
_____
2PM_____
_____
3PM_____
_____
4PM_____
_____
5PM_____
_____
6PM_____
_____

THURSDAY	FRIDAY	SATURDAY	Goals
5AM_____	5AM_____	9AM_____	
_____	_____	_____	_____
6AM_____	6AM_____	10AM_____	_____
_____	_____	_____	_____
7AM_____	7AM_____	11AM_____	_____
_____	_____	_____	_____
8AM_____	8AM_____	12PM_____	_____
_____	_____	_____	_____
9AM_____	9AM_____	1PM_____	_____
_____	_____	_____	_____
10AM_____	10AM_____	2PM_____	_____
_____	_____	_____	
11AM_____	11AM_____	3PM_____	
_____	_____	_____	
12PM_____	12PM_____	4PM_____	
_____	_____	_____	
1PM_____	1PM_____	5PM_____	
_____	_____	_____	
2PM_____	2PM_____	6PM_____	Action Steps
_____	_____	_____	
3PM_____	3PM_____		
_____	_____		_____
4PM_____	4PM_____		_____
_____	_____		_____
5PM_____	5PM_____		_____
_____	_____	"What area of the	_____
6PM_____	6PM_____	Life Wheel would	_____
_____	_____	you choose to work	_____
7PM_____	7PM_____	with first?" p. 18	_____
_____	_____		_____
8PM_____	8PM_____		_____
_____	_____		_____

WEEK OF _____ TO _____

Areas of my Life
Wheel on my radar

_____

_____

_____

_____

MONDAY	TUESDAY	WEDNESDAY
5AM_____	5AM_____	5AM_____
6AM_____	6AM_____	6AM_____
7AM_____	7AM_____	7AM_____
8AM_____	8AM_____	8AM_____
9AM_____	9AM_____	9AM_____
10AM_____	10AM_____	10AM_____
11AM_____	11AM_____	11AM_____
12PM_____	12PM_____	12PM_____
1PM_____	1PM_____	1PM_____
2PM_____	2PM_____	2PM_____
3PM_____	3PM_____	3PM_____
4PM_____	4PM_____	4PM_____
5PM_____	5PM_____	5PM_____
6PM_____	6PM_____	6PM_____
7PM_____	7PM_____	7PM_____
8PM_____	8PM_____	8PM_____

SUNDAY

9AM_____

10AM_____

11AM_____

12PM_____

1PM_____

2PM_____

3PM_____

4PM_____

5PM_____

6PM_____

THURSDAY	FRIDAY	SATURDAY
5AM_____	5AM_____	9AM_____
6AM_____	6AM_____	10AM_____
7AM_____	7AM_____	11AM_____
8AM_____	8AM_____	12PM_____
9AM_____	9AM_____	1PM_____
10AM_____	10AM_____	2PM_____
11AM_____	11AM_____	3PM_____
12PM_____	12PM_____	4PM_____
1PM_____	1PM_____	5PM_____
2PM_____	2PM_____	6PM_____
3PM_____	3PM_____	
4PM_____	4PM_____	
5PM_____	5PM_____	"I choose to assess what's on my radar and my Life Wheel to see the real condition of my life." p. 21
6PM_____	6PM_____	
7PM_____	7PM_____	
8PM_____	8PM_____	

Goals

_____
_____
_____
_____
_____
_____
_____

Action Steps

_____
_____
_____
_____
_____
_____
_____

WEEK OF _____ TO _____

Areas of my Life Wheel on my radar

_____

_____

_____

_____

MONDAY	TUESDAY	WEDNESDAY
5AM_____	5AM_____	5AM_____
_____	_____	_____
6AM_____	6AM_____	6AM_____
_____	_____	_____
7AM_____	7AM_____	7AM_____
_____	_____	_____
8AM_____	8AM_____	8AM_____
_____	_____	_____
9AM_____	9AM_____	9AM_____
_____	_____	_____
10AM_____	10AM_____	10AM_____
_____	_____	_____
11AM_____	11AM_____	11AM_____
_____	_____	_____
12PM_____	12PM_____	12PM_____
_____	_____	_____
1PM_____	1PM_____	1PM_____
_____	_____	_____
2PM_____	2PM_____	2PM_____
_____	_____	_____
3PM_____	3PM_____	3PM_____
_____	_____	_____
4PM_____	4PM_____	4PM_____
_____	_____	_____
5PM_____	5PM_____	5PM_____
_____	_____	_____
6PM_____	6PM_____	6PM_____
_____	_____	_____
7PM_____	7PM_____	7PM_____
_____	_____	_____
8PM_____	8PM_____	8PM_____
_____	_____	_____

SUNDAY

9AM_____

_____

10AM_____

_____

11AM_____

_____

12PM_____

_____

1PM_____

_____

2PM_____

_____

3PM_____

_____

4PM_____

_____

5PM_____

_____

6PM_____

_____

THURSDAY	FRIDAY	SATURDAY	Goals
5AM _____	5AM _____	9AM _____	_____
6AM _____	6AM _____	10AM _____	_____
7AM _____	7AM _____	11AM _____	_____
8AM _____	8AM _____	12PM _____	_____
9AM _____	9AM _____	1PM _____	_____
10AM _____	10AM _____	2PM _____	_____
11AM _____	11AM _____	3PM _____	_____
12PM _____	12PM _____	4PM _____	
1PM _____	1PM _____	5PM _____	
2PM _____	2PM _____	6PM _____	**Action Steps**
3PM _____	3PM _____		_____
4PM _____	4PM _____		_____
5PM _____	5PM _____	"I choose to take action to increase my satisfaction in one area of my Life Wheel." p. 21	_____
6PM _____	6PM _____		_____
7PM _____	7PM _____		_____
8PM _____	8PM _____		_____

WEEK OF _____ TO _____

Areas of my Life
Wheel on my radar

_____

_____

_____

_____

SUNDAY	MONDAY	TUESDAY	WEDNESDAY
9AM_____	5AM_____	5AM_____	5AM_____
_____	_____	_____	_____
10AM_____	6AM_____	6AM_____	6AM_____
_____	_____	_____	_____
11AM_____	7AM_____	7AM_____	7AM_____
_____	_____	_____	_____
12PM_____	8AM_____	8AM_____	8AM_____
_____	_____	_____	_____
1PM_____	9AM_____	9AM_____	9AM_____
_____	_____	_____	_____
2PM_____	10AM_____	10AM_____	10AM_____
_____	_____	_____	_____
3PM_____	11AM_____	11AM_____	11AM_____
_____	_____	_____	_____
4PM_____	12PM_____	12PM_____	12PM_____
_____	_____	_____	_____
5PM_____	1PM_____	1PM_____	1PM_____
_____	_____	_____	_____
6PM_____	2PM_____	2PM_____	2PM_____
_____	_____	_____	_____
	3PM_____	3PM_____	3PM_____
	_____	_____	_____
	4PM_____	4PM_____	4PM_____
	_____	_____	_____
	5PM_____	5PM_____	5PM_____
	_____	_____	_____
	6PM_____	6PM_____	6PM_____
	_____	_____	_____
	7PM_____	7PM_____	7PM_____
	_____	_____	_____
	8PM_____	8PM_____	8PM_____
	_____	_____	_____

THURSDAY	FRIDAY	SATURDAY
5AM_____	5AM_____	9AM_____
6AM_____	6AM_____	10AM_____
7AM_____	7AM_____	11AM_____
8AM_____	8AM_____	12PM_____
9AM_____	9AM_____	1PM_____
10AM_____	10AM_____	2PM_____
11AM_____	11AM_____	3PM_____
12PM_____	12PM_____	4PM_____
1PM_____	1PM_____	5PM_____
2PM_____	2PM_____	6PM_____
3PM_____	3PM_____	
4PM_____	4PM_____	
5PM_____	5PM_____	
6PM_____	6PM_____	"Every day we utilize a set of filters acquired from our experiences and life stories." p. 24
7PM_____	7PM_____	
8PM_____	8PM_____	

Goals

_____
_____
_____
_____
_____
_____
_____

Action Steps

_____
_____
_____
_____
_____
_____
_____

WEEK OF _____ TO _____

Areas of my Life Wheel on my radar

_____

_____

_____

_____

SUNDAY

9AM_____
_____
10AM_____
_____
11AM_____
_____
12PM_____
_____
1PM_____
_____
2PM_____
_____
3PM_____
_____
4PM_____
_____
5PM_____
_____
6PM_____
_____

MONDAY

5AM_____
_____
6AM_____
_____
7AM_____
_____
8AM_____
_____
9AM_____
_____
10AM_____
_____
11AM_____
_____
12PM_____
_____
1PM_____
_____
2PM_____
_____
3PM_____
_____
4PM_____
_____
5PM_____
_____
6PM_____
_____
7PM_____
_____
8PM_____
_____

TUESDAY

5AM_____
_____
6AM_____
_____
7AM_____
_____
8AM_____
_____
9AM_____
_____
10AM_____
_____
11AM_____
_____
12PM_____
_____
1PM_____
_____
2PM_____
_____
3PM_____
_____
4PM_____
_____
5PM_____
_____
6PM_____
_____
7PM_____
_____
8PM_____
_____

WEDNESDAY

5AM_____
_____
6AM_____
_____
7AM_____
_____
8AM_____
_____
9AM_____
_____
10AM_____
_____
11AM_____
_____
12PM_____
_____
1PM_____
_____
2PM_____
_____
3PM_____
_____
4PM_____
_____
5PM_____
_____
6PM_____
_____
7PM_____
_____
8PM_____
_____

THURSDAY	FRIDAY	SATURDAY
5AM_____	5AM_____	9AM_____
6AM_____	6AM_____	10AM_____
7AM_____	7AM_____	11AM_____
8AM_____	8AM_____	12PM_____
9AM_____	9AM_____	1PM_____
10AM_____	10AM_____	2PM_____
11AM_____	11AM_____	3PM_____
12PM_____	12PM_____	4PM_____
1PM_____	1PM_____	5PM_____
2PM_____	2PM_____	6PM_____
3PM_____	3PM_____	
4PM_____	4PM_____	
5PM_____	5PM_____	
6PM_____	6PM_____	
7PM_____	7PM_____	
8PM_____	8PM_____	

"The layers you are beginning to reveal about yourself are more obvious to everyone around you than you realize, and you're unaware of the impact of the message and presence you exude." p. 31

Goals

_____
_____
_____
_____
_____
_____
_____

Action Steps

_____
_____
_____
_____
_____
_____
_____

NOTES_____

NOTES_____

MONTHLY SELF-REFLECTION:
Measuring the Net Value of Our Choices

What did you discover about yourself from the previous Life Wheel exercise? In what ways did that discovery surprise you? What specific awareness or revelations are most valuable to you?

_____
_____
_____
_____

Which area(s) did you focus on last month? Why?

_____
_____
_____
_____

How were your action steps effective or ineffective? What will you add, alter, or remove about those action steps going forward?

_____
_____
_____
_____

In what ways did having this awareness improve your personal life? Your professional life? The way you lead others?

_____
_____
_____
_____

Knowing we all fall short and have moments we don't achieve our goals and expectations, how will you extend grace to yourself to move forward?

_____
_____
_____
_____

Monthly Life Wheel Exercise

* Feel free to change or add an area. If it's important to you, it's important.

On a scale of one to ten, one being the lowest of the low and ten being best, rate your level of fulfillment in each category and record on the Life Wheel.

Business Calling _____   Financial Health _____

Physical Wellness _____   Relational Health _____

Intimacy _____   Personal Development _____

Play Time/Fun _____   Spiritual Wellness _____

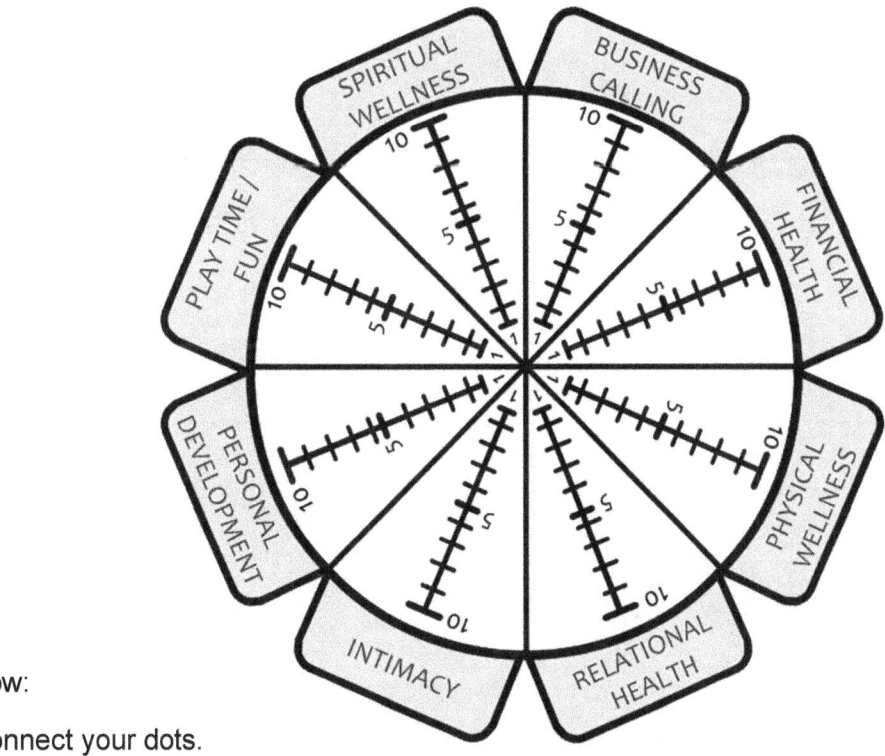

Now:

Connect your dots.

Determine what's on your radar.

What action steps can you take for improvement?

Record your action steps on your month overview. Reassess your steps each week and update accordingly using the central question: In this moment, what choice can I make and what action can I take to create the greatest net value?

Life Wheel Focus Area: *Business Calling: Internal Perspective*
What about this area is important to me?

_____

_____

MONTH: _____   YEAR: _____

Action Steps

_____
_____
_____
_____
_____
_____
_____
_____
_____
_____

OPPORTUNITIES

- [ ] _____
- [ ] _____
- [ ] _____
- [ ] _____
- [ ] _____
- [ ] _____
- [ ] _____
- [ ] _____
- [ ] _____
- [ ] _____

SUNDAY	MONDAY	TUESDAY

NOTES:

How does this verse apply to my internal world?

_____

WEDNESDAY	THURSDAY	FRIDAY	SATURDAY

"Every individual has their very own, personal onion to slay." p. 16

WEEK OF _____ TO _____

Areas of my Life Wheel on my radar	MONDAY	TUESDAY	WEDNESDAY
_____	5AM_____	5AM_____	5AM_____
_____	6AM_____	6AM_____	6AM_____
_____	7AM_____	7AM_____	7AM_____
_____	8AM_____	8AM_____	8AM_____
	9AM_____	9AM_____	9AM_____
SUNDAY	10AM_____	10AM_____	10AM_____
9AM_____	11AM_____	11AM_____	11AM_____
10AM_____	12PM_____	12PM_____	12PM_____
11AM_____	1PM_____	1PM_____	1PM_____
12PM_____	2PM_____	2PM_____	2PM_____
1PM_____	3PM_____	3PM_____	3PM_____
2PM_____	4PM_____	4PM_____	4PM_____
3PM_____	5PM_____	5PM_____	5PM_____
4PM_____	6PM_____	6PM_____	6PM_____
5PM_____	7PM_____	7PM_____	7PM_____
6PM_____	8PM_____	8PM_____	8PM_____

THURSDAY	FRIDAY	SATURDAY
5AM_____	5AM_____	9AM_____
6AM_____	6AM_____	10AM_____
7AM_____	7AM_____	11AM_____
8AM_____	8AM_____	12PM_____
9AM_____	9AM_____	1PM_____
10AM_____	10AM_____	2PM_____
11AM_____	11AM_____	3PM_____
12PM_____	12PM_____	4PM_____
1PM_____	1PM_____	5PM_____
2PM_____	2PM_____	6PM_____
3PM_____	3PM_____	
4PM_____	4PM_____	
5PM_____	5PM_____	"I choose to give myself grace as I need it without beating up on myself." p. 21
6PM_____	6PM_____	
7PM_____	7PM_____	
8PM_____	8PM_____	

Goals

_____
_____
_____
_____
_____
_____
_____

Action Steps

_____
_____
_____
_____
_____
_____
_____

WEEK OF _____ TO _____

Areas of my Life Wheel on my radar

_____

_____

_____

_____

MONDAY	TUESDAY	WEDNESDAY
5AM_____	5AM_____	5AM_____
_____	_____	_____
6AM_____	6AM_____	6AM_____
_____	_____	_____
7AM_____	7AM_____	7AM_____
_____	_____	_____
8AM_____	8AM_____	8AM_____
_____	_____	_____
9AM_____	9AM_____	9AM_____
_____	_____	_____
10AM_____	10AM_____	10AM_____
_____	_____	_____
11AM_____	11AM_____	11AM_____
_____	_____	_____
12PM_____	12PM_____	12PM_____
_____	_____	_____
1PM_____	1PM_____	1PM_____
_____	_____	_____
2PM_____	2PM_____	2PM_____
_____	_____	_____
3PM_____	3PM_____	3PM_____
_____	_____	_____
4PM_____	4PM_____	4PM_____
_____	_____	_____
5PM_____	5PM_____	5PM_____
_____	_____	_____
6PM_____	6PM_____	6PM_____
_____	_____	_____
7PM_____	7PM_____	7PM_____
_____	_____	_____
8PM_____	8PM_____	8PM_____
_____	_____	_____

SUNDAY

9AM_____

_____

10AM_____

_____

11AM_____

_____

12PM_____

_____

1PM_____

_____

2PM_____

_____

3PM_____

_____

4PM_____

_____

5PM_____

_____

6PM_____

_____

THURSDAY	FRIDAY	SATURDAY
5AM_____	5AM_____	9AM_____
6AM_____	6AM_____	10AM_____
7AM_____	7AM_____	11AM_____
8AM_____	8AM_____	12PM_____
9AM_____	9AM_____	1PM_____
10AM_____	10AM_____	2PM_____
11AM_____	11AM_____	3PM_____
12PM_____	12PM_____	4PM_____
1PM_____	1PM_____	5PM_____
2PM_____	2PM_____	6PM_____
3PM_____	3PM_____	
4PM_____	4PM_____	
5PM_____	5PM_____	"Many of us don't know how to look in the mirror, face our fears, and challenge ourselves to leave our comfort zones, whether they are healthy or unhealthy in nature." p. 7
6PM_____	6PM_____	
7PM_____	7PM_____	
8PM_____	8PM_____	

Goals

_____
_____
_____
_____
_____
_____
_____

Action Steps

_____
_____
_____
_____
_____
_____
_____

WEEK OF _____ TO _____

Areas of my Life
Wheel on my radar

_____

_____

_____

_____

SUNDAY	MONDAY	TUESDAY	WEDNESDAY
9AM_____	5AM_____	5AM_____	5AM_____
10AM_____	6AM_____	6AM_____	6AM_____
11AM_____	7AM_____	7AM_____	7AM_____
12PM_____	8AM_____	8AM_____	8AM_____
1PM_____	9AM_____	9AM_____	9AM_____
2PM_____	10AM_____	10AM_____	10AM_____
3PM_____	11AM_____	11AM_____	11AM_____
4PM_____	12PM_____	12PM_____	12PM_____
5PM_____	1PM_____	1PM_____	1PM_____
6PM_____	2PM_____	2PM_____	2PM_____
	3PM_____	3PM_____	3PM_____
	4PM_____	4PM_____	4PM_____
	5PM_____	5PM_____	5PM_____
	6PM_____	6PM_____	6PM_____
	7PM_____	7PM_____	7PM_____
	8PM_____	8PM_____	8PM_____

THURSDAY	FRIDAY	SATURDAY
5AM	5AM	9AM
6AM	6AM	10AM
7AM	7AM	11AM
8AM	8AM	12PM
9AM	9AM	1PM
10AM	10AM	2PM
11AM	11AM	3PM
12PM	12PM	4PM
1PM	1PM	5PM
2PM	2PM	6PM
3PM	3PM	
4PM	4PM	
5PM	5PM	
6PM	6PM	"Be faithful to yourself." p. 20
7PM	7PM	
8PM	8PM	

Goals

Action Steps

WEEK OF _____ TO _____

Areas of my Life Wheel on my radar

_____

_____

_____

_____

SUNDAY

9AM_____

_____

10AM_____

_____

11AM_____

_____

12PM_____

_____

1PM_____

_____

2PM_____

_____

3PM_____

_____

4PM_____

_____

5PM_____

_____

6PM_____

_____

MONDAY

5AM_____

_____

6AM_____

_____

7AM_____

_____

8AM_____

_____

9AM_____

_____

10AM_____

_____

11AM_____

_____

12PM_____

_____

1PM_____

_____

2PM_____

_____

3PM_____

_____

4PM_____

_____

5PM_____

_____

6PM_____

_____

7PM_____

_____

8PM_____

_____

TUESDAY

5AM_____

_____

6AM_____

_____

7AM_____

_____

8AM_____

_____

9AM_____

_____

10AM_____

_____

11AM_____

_____

12PM_____

_____

1PM_____

_____

2PM_____

_____

3PM_____

_____

4PM_____

_____

5PM_____

_____

6PM_____

_____

7PM_____

_____

8PM_____

_____

WEDNESDAY

5AM_____

_____

6AM_____

_____

7AM_____

_____

8AM_____

_____

9AM_____

_____

10AM_____

_____

11AM_____

_____

12PM_____

_____

1PM_____

_____

2PM_____

_____

3PM_____

_____

4PM_____

_____

5PM_____

_____

6PM_____

_____

7PM_____

_____

8PM_____

_____

THURSDAY	FRIDAY	SATURDAY
5AM_____	5AM_____	9AM_____
6AM_____	6AM_____	10AM_____
7AM_____	7AM_____	11AM_____
8AM_____	8AM_____	12PM_____
9AM_____	9AM_____	1PM_____
10AM_____	10AM_____	2PM_____
11AM_____	11AM_____	3PM_____
12PM_____	12PM_____	4PM_____
1PM_____	1PM_____	5PM_____
2PM_____	2PM_____	6PM_____
3PM_____	3PM_____	
4PM_____	4PM_____	"Choosing to be transparent, vulnerable, and approachable in a surface-layer world is risky, but it can also be deeply rewarding once we learn the process and its benefits." p. 36
5PM_____	5PM_____	
6PM_____	6PM_____	
7PM_____	7PM_____	
8PM_____	8PM_____	

Goals

_____
_____
_____
_____
_____
_____
_____

Action Steps

_____
_____
_____
_____
_____
_____
_____

WEEK OF _____ TO _____

Areas of my Life
Wheel on my radar

_____

_____

_____

_____

SUNDAY

9AM_____

_____

10AM_____

_____

11AM_____

_____

12PM_____

_____

1PM_____

_____

2PM_____

_____

3PM_____

_____

4PM_____

_____

5PM_____

_____

6PM_____

_____

MONDAY

5AM_____

_____

6AM_____

_____

7AM_____

_____

8AM_____

_____

9AM_____

_____

10AM_____

_____

11AM_____

_____

12PM_____

_____

1PM_____

_____

2PM_____

_____

3PM_____

_____

4PM_____

_____

5PM_____

_____

6PM_____

_____

7PM_____

_____

8PM_____

_____

TUESDAY

5AM_____

_____

6AM_____

_____

7AM_____

_____

8AM_____

_____

9AM_____

_____

10AM_____

_____

11AM_____

_____

12PM_____

_____

1PM_____

_____

2PM_____

_____

3PM_____

_____

4PM_____

_____

5PM_____

_____

6PM_____

_____

7PM_____

_____

8PM_____

_____

WEDNESDAY

5AM_____

_____

6AM_____

_____

7AM_____

_____

8AM_____

_____

9AM_____

_____

10AM_____

_____

11AM_____

_____

12PM_____

_____

1PM_____

_____

2PM_____

_____

3PM_____

_____

4PM_____

_____

5PM_____

_____

6PM_____

_____

7PM_____

_____

8PM_____

_____

THURSDAY	FRIDAY	SATURDAY
5AM_____	5AM_____	9AM_____
_____	_____	_____
6AM_____	6AM_____	10AM_____
_____	_____	_____
7AM_____	7AM_____	11AM_____
_____	_____	_____
8AM_____	8AM_____	12PM_____
_____	_____	_____
9AM_____	9AM_____	1PM_____
_____	_____	_____
10AM_____	10AM_____	2PM_____
_____	_____	_____
11AM_____	11AM_____	3PM_____
_____	_____	_____
12PM_____	12PM_____	4PM_____
_____	_____	_____
1PM_____	1PM_____	5PM_____
_____	_____	_____
2PM_____	2PM_____	6PM_____
_____	_____	_____
3PM_____	3PM_____	
_____	_____	
4PM_____	4PM_____	
_____	_____	
5PM_____	5PM_____	
_____	_____	"What we love affects all areas of our lives. Every. Single. Layer." p. 47
6PM_____	6PM_____	
_____	_____	
7PM_____	7PM_____	
_____	_____	
8PM_____	8PM_____	
_____	_____	

Goals

_____

_____

_____

_____

_____

_____

_____

Action Steps

_____

_____

_____

_____

_____

_____

_____

NOTES

NOTES_____
_____
_____
_____
_____
_____
_____
_____
_____
_____
_____
_____
_____
_____
_____
_____
_____
_____
_____
_____
_____
_____
_____
_____
_____
_____
_____
_____
_____
_____
_____
_____
_____
_____
_____

MONTHLY SELF-REFLECTION:
Measuring the Net Value of Our Choices

What did you discover about yourself from the previous Life Wheel exercise? In what ways did that discovery surprise you? What specific awareness or revelations are most valuable to you?

_____
_____
_____
_____

Which area(s) did you focus on last month? Why?

_____
_____
_____
_____

How were your action steps effective or ineffective? What will you add, alter, or remove about those action steps going forward?

_____
_____
_____
_____

In what ways did having this awareness improve your personal life? Your professional life? The way you lead others?

_____
_____
_____
_____

Knowing we all fall short and have moments we don't achieve our goals and expectations, how will you extend grace to yourself to move forward?

_____
_____
_____
_____

Monthly Life Wheel Exercise

* Feel free to change or add an area. If it's important to you, it's important.

On a scale of one to ten, one being the lowest of the low and ten being best, rate your level of fulfillment in each category and record on the Life Wheel.

Business Calling _____   Financial Health _____

Physical Wellness _____   Relational Health _____

Intimacy _____   Personal Development _____

Play Time/Fun _____   Spiritual Wellness _____

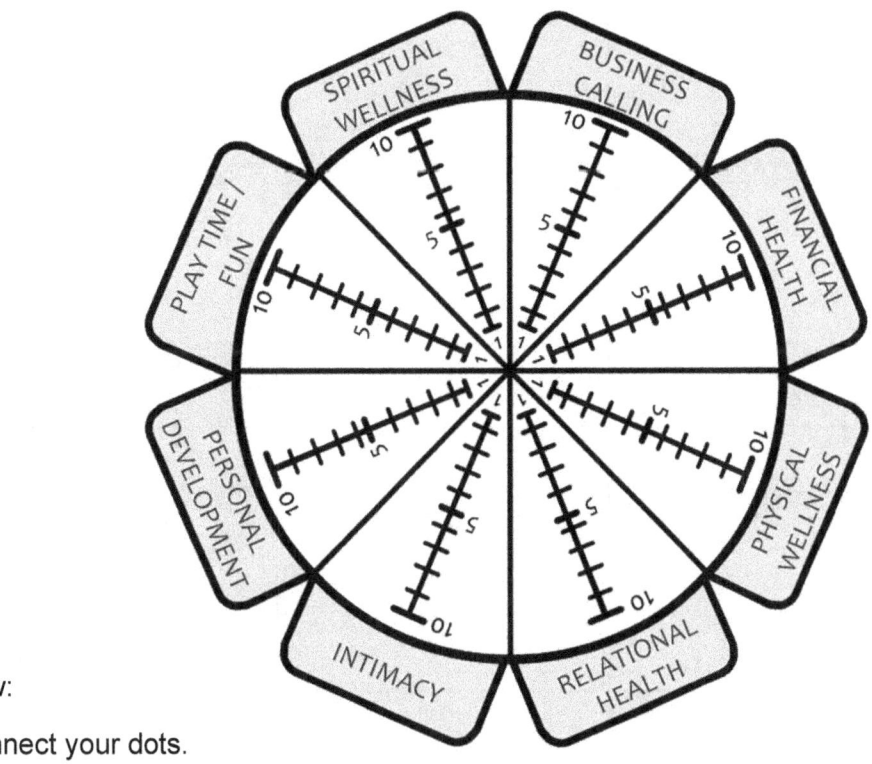

Now:

Connect your dots.

Determine what's on your radar.

What action steps can you take for improvement?

Record your action steps on your month overview. Reassess your steps each week and update accordingly using the central question: In this moment, what choice can I make and what action can I take to create the greatest net value?

Life Wheel Focus Area: *Financial Health: External Perspective*
What about this area is important to me?

_____

_____

MONTH: _____ YEAR: _____

Action Steps

_____
_____
_____
_____
_____
_____
_____
_____
_____
_____
_____
_____

OPPORTUNITIES

- ☐ _____
- ☐ _____
- ☐ _____
- ☐ _____
- ☐ _____
- ☐ _____
- ☐ _____
- ☐ _____
- ☐ _____
- ☐ _____

SUNDAY	MONDAY	TUESDAY

NOTES:

Focus Verse: "Suppose one of you wants to build a tower. Won't you first sit down and estimate the cost to see if you have enough money to complete it?" Luke 14:28
How does this verse apply to my external world?

_____

WEDNESDAY	THURSDAY	FRIDAY	SATURDAY

"I choose to recognize the implications of investing in relationships." p. 144

WEEK OF _____ TO _____

Areas of my Life Wheel on my radar

_____

_____

_____

_____

MONDAY	TUESDAY	WEDNESDAY
5AM_____	5AM_____	5AM_____
6AM_____	6AM_____	6AM_____
7AM_____	7AM_____	7AM_____
8AM_____	8AM_____	8AM_____
9AM_____	9AM_____	9AM_____
10AM_____	10AM_____	10AM_____
11AM_____	11AM_____	11AM_____
12PM_____	12PM_____	12PM_____
1PM_____	1PM_____	1PM_____
2PM_____	2PM_____	2PM_____
3PM_____	3PM_____	3PM_____
4PM_____	4PM_____	4PM_____
5PM_____	5PM_____	5PM_____
6PM_____	6PM_____	6PM_____
7PM_____	7PM_____	7PM_____
8PM_____	8PM_____	8PM_____

SUNDAY

9AM_____

10AM_____

11AM_____

12PM_____

1PM_____

2PM_____

3PM_____

4PM_____

5PM_____

6PM_____

THURSDAY	FRIDAY	SATURDAY
5AM _____	5AM _____	9AM _____
6AM _____	6AM _____	10AM _____
7AM _____	7AM _____	11AM _____
8AM _____	8AM _____	12PM _____
9AM _____	9AM _____	1PM _____
10AM _____	10AM _____	2PM _____
11AM _____	11AM _____	3PM _____
12PM _____	12PM _____	4PM _____
1PM _____	1PM _____	5PM _____
2PM _____	2PM _____	6PM _____
3PM _____	3PM _____	
4PM _____	4PM _____	
5PM _____	5PM _____	"I choose to understand as I slay each layer it may reveal another layer." p. 21
6PM _____	6PM _____	
7PM _____	7PM _____	
8PM _____	8PM _____	

Goals

_____
_____
_____
_____
_____
_____

Action Steps

_____
_____
_____
_____
_____
_____

WEEK OF _____ TO _____

Areas of my Life
Wheel on my radar

_____

_____

_____

_____

MONDAY	TUESDAY	WEDNESDAY
5AM_____	5AM_____	5AM_____
6AM_____	6AM_____	6AM_____
7AM_____	7AM_____	7AM_____
8AM_____	8AM_____	8AM_____
9AM_____	9AM_____	9AM_____
10AM_____	10AM_____	10AM_____
11AM_____	11AM_____	11AM_____
12PM_____	12PM_____	12PM_____
1PM_____	1PM_____	1PM_____
2PM_____	2PM_____	2PM_____
3PM_____	3PM_____	3PM_____
4PM_____	4PM_____	4PM_____
5PM_____	5PM_____	5PM_____
6PM_____	6PM_____	6PM_____
7PM_____	7PM_____	7PM_____
8PM_____	8PM_____	8PM_____

SUNDAY

9AM_____

10AM_____

11AM_____

12PM_____

1PM_____

2PM_____

3PM_____

4PM_____

5PM_____

6PM_____

THURSDAY	FRIDAY	SATURDAY
5AM_____	5AM_____	9AM_____
6AM_____	6AM_____	10AM_____
7AM_____	7AM_____	11AM_____
8AM_____	8AM_____	12PM_____
9AM_____	9AM_____	1PM_____
10AM_____	10AM_____	2PM_____
11AM_____	11AM_____	3PM_____
12PM_____	12PM_____	4PM_____
1PM_____	1PM_____	5PM_____
2PM_____	2PM_____	6PM_____
3PM_____	3PM_____	
4PM_____	4PM_____	
5PM_____	5PM_____	"Our history affects how we identify, present, and perceive ourselves." p. 39
6PM_____	6PM_____	
7PM_____	7PM_____	
8PM_____	8PM_____	

Goals

_____
_____
_____
_____
_____
_____
_____

Action Steps

_____
_____
_____
_____
_____
_____
_____

WEEK OF _____ TO _____

Areas of my Life Wheel on my radar

_____

_____

_____

_____

SUNDAY

9AM_____

_____

10AM_____

_____

11AM_____

_____

12PM_____

_____

1PM_____

_____

2PM_____

_____

3PM_____

_____

4PM_____

_____

5PM_____

_____

6PM_____

_____

MONDAY

5AM_____

_____

6AM_____

_____

7AM_____

_____

8AM_____

_____

9AM_____

_____

10AM_____

_____

11AM_____

_____

12PM_____

_____

1PM_____

_____

2PM_____

_____

3PM_____

_____

4PM_____

_____

5PM_____

_____

6PM_____

_____

7PM_____

_____

8PM_____

_____

TUESDAY

5AM_____

_____

6AM_____

_____

7AM_____

_____

8AM_____

_____

9AM_____

_____

10AM_____

_____

11AM_____

_____

12PM_____

_____

1PM_____

_____

2PM_____

_____

3PM_____

_____

4PM_____

_____

5PM_____

_____

6PM_____

_____

7PM_____

_____

8PM_____

_____

WEDNESDAY

5AM_____

_____

6AM_____

_____

7AM_____

_____

8AM_____

_____

9AM_____

_____

10AM_____

_____

11AM_____

_____

12PM_____

_____

1PM_____

_____

2PM_____

_____

3PM_____

_____

4PM_____

_____

5PM_____

_____

6PM_____

_____

7PM_____

_____

8PM_____

_____

THURSDAY	FRIDAY	SATURDAY
5AM_____	5AM_____	9AM_____
6AM_____	6AM_____	10AM_____
7AM_____	7AM_____	11AM_____
8AM_____	8AM_____	12PM_____
9AM_____	9AM_____	1PM_____
10AM_____	10AM_____	2PM_____
11AM_____	11AM_____	3PM_____
12PM_____	12PM_____	4PM_____
1PM_____	1PM_____	5PM_____
2PM_____	2PM_____	6PM_____
3PM_____	3PM_____	
4PM_____	4PM_____	
5PM_____	5PM_____	
6PM_____	6PM_____	"We all use our memories to derive our identities." p. 43
7PM_____	7PM_____	
8PM_____	8PM_____	

Goals

_____
_____
_____
_____
_____
_____
_____

Action Steps

_____
_____
_____
_____
_____
_____

WEEK OF _____ TO _____

Areas of my Life
Wheel on my radar

_____

_____

_____

_____

MONDAY	TUESDAY	WEDNESDAY
5AM_____	5AM_____	5AM_____
6AM_____	6AM_____	6AM_____
7AM_____	7AM_____	7AM_____
8AM_____	8AM_____	8AM_____
9AM_____	9AM_____	9AM_____
10AM_____	10AM_____	10AM_____
11AM_____	11AM_____	11AM_____
12PM_____	12PM_____	12PM_____
1PM_____	1PM_____	1PM_____
2PM_____	2PM_____	2PM_____
3PM_____	3PM_____	3PM_____
4PM_____	4PM_____	4PM_____
5PM_____	5PM_____	5PM_____
6PM_____	6PM_____	6PM_____
7PM_____	7PM_____	7PM_____
8PM_____	8PM_____	8PM_____

SUNDAY

9AM_____

10AM_____

11AM_____

12PM_____

1PM_____

2PM_____

3PM_____

4PM_____

5PM_____

6PM_____

THURSDAY	FRIDAY	SATURDAY
5AM_____	5AM_____	9AM_____
6AM_____	6AM_____	10AM_____
7AM_____	7AM_____	11AM_____
8AM_____	8AM_____	12PM_____
9AM_____	9AM_____	1PM_____
10AM_____	10AM_____	2PM_____
11AM_____	11AM_____	3PM_____
12PM_____	12PM_____	4PM_____
1PM_____	1PM_____	5PM_____
2PM_____	2PM_____	6PM_____
3PM_____	3PM_____	
4PM_____	4PM_____	
5PM_____	5PM_____	"We all wear an invisible mask of our external and internal perspectives." p.36
6PM_____	6PM_____	
7PM_____	7PM_____	
8PM_____	8PM_____	

Goals

_____
_____
_____
_____
_____
_____

Action Steps

_____
_____
_____
_____
_____
_____
_____

WEEK OF _____ TO _____

Areas of my Life Wheel on my radar

_____

_____

_____

_____

SUNDAY

9AM_____
_____
10AM_____
_____
11AM_____
_____
12PM_____
_____
1PM_____
_____
2PM_____
_____
3PM_____
_____
4PM_____
_____
5PM_____
_____
6PM_____
_____

MONDAY

5AM_____
_____
6AM_____
_____
7AM_____
_____
8AM_____
_____
9AM_____
_____
10AM_____
_____
11AM_____
_____
12PM_____
_____
1PM_____
_____
2PM_____
_____
3PM_____
_____
4PM_____
_____
5PM_____
_____
6PM_____
_____
7PM_____
_____
8PM_____
_____

TUESDAY

5AM_____
_____
6AM_____
_____
7AM_____
_____
8AM_____
_____
9AM_____
_____
10AM_____
_____
11AM_____
_____
12PM_____
_____
1PM_____
_____
2PM_____
_____
3PM_____
_____
4PM_____
_____
5PM_____
_____
6PM_____
_____
7PM_____
_____
8PM_____
_____

WEDNESDAY

5AM_____
_____
6AM_____
_____
7AM_____
_____
8AM_____
_____
9AM_____
_____
10AM_____
_____
11AM_____
_____
12PM_____
_____
1PM_____
_____
2PM_____
_____
3PM_____
_____
4PM_____
_____
5PM_____
_____
6PM_____
_____
7PM_____
_____
8PM_____
_____

THURSDAY	FRIDAY	SATURDAY
5AM_____	5AM_____	9AM_____
_____	_____	_____
6AM_____	6AM_____	10AM_____
_____	_____	_____
7AM_____	7AM_____	11AM_____
_____	_____	_____
8AM_____	8AM_____	12PM_____
_____	_____	_____
9AM_____	9AM_____	1PM_____
_____	_____	_____
10AM_____	10AM_____	2PM_____
_____	_____	_____
11AM_____	11AM_____	3PM_____
_____	_____	_____
12PM_____	12PM_____	4PM_____
_____	_____	_____
1PM_____	1PM_____	5PM_____
_____	_____	_____
2PM_____	2PM_____	6PM_____
_____	_____	_____
3PM_____	3PM_____	
4PM_____	4PM_____	
_____	_____	
5PM_____	5PM_____	
_____	_____	"I choose to operate in quiet leadership with myself and others." p. 144
6PM_____	6PM_____	
_____	_____	
7PM_____	7PM_____	
_____	_____	
8PM_____	8PM_____	
_____	_____	

Goals

_____
_____
_____
_____
_____
_____
_____

Action Steps

_____
_____
_____
_____
_____
_____
_____
_____

NOTES_____
_____
_____
_____
_____
_____
_____
_____
_____
_____
_____
_____
_____
_____
_____
_____
_____
_____
_____
_____
_____
_____
_____
_____
_____
_____
_____
_____
_____
_____
_____
_____
_____
_____
_____
_____

NOTES

MONTHLY SELF-REFLECTION:
Measuring the Net Value of Our Choices

What did you discover about yourself from the previous Life Wheel exercise? In what ways did that discovery surprise you? What specific awareness or revelations are most valuable to you?

_____

_____

_____

_____

Which area(s) did you focus on last month? Why?

_____

_____

_____

_____

How were your action steps effective or ineffective? What will you add, alter, or remove about those action steps going forward?

_____

_____

_____

_____

In what ways did having this awareness improve your personal life? Your professional life? The way you lead others?

_____

_____

_____

_____

Knowing we all fall short and have moments we don't achieve our goals and expectations, how will you extend grace to yourself to move forward?

_____

_____

_____

_____

Monthly Life Wheel Exercise

* Feel free to change or add an area. If it's important to you, it's important.

On a scale of one to ten, one being the lowest of the low and ten being best, rate your level of fulfillment in each category and record on the Life Wheel.

Business Calling _____   Financial Health _____

Physical Wellness _____   Relational Health _____

Intimacy _____   Personal Development _____

Play Time/Fun _____   Spiritual Wellness _____

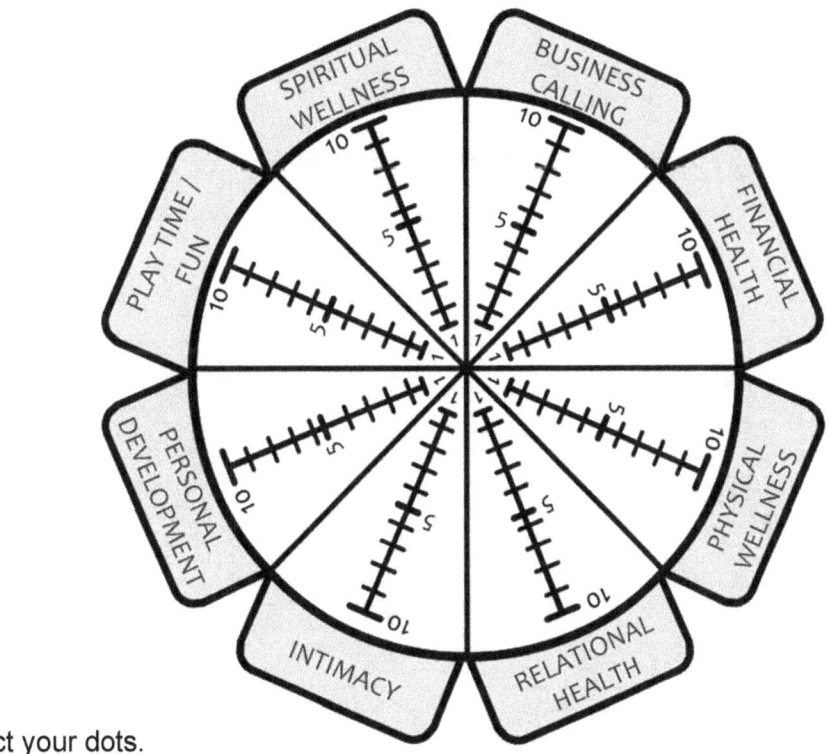

Now:

Connect your dots.

Determine what's on your radar.

What action steps can you take for improvement?

Record your action steps on your month overview. Reassess your steps each week and update accordingly using the central question: In this moment, what choice can I make and what action can I take to create the greatest net value?

Life Wheel Focus Area: *Financial Health: Internal Perspective*

What about this area is important to me?

_____

_____

MONTH: _____   YEAR: _____

Action Steps

_____
_____
_____
_____
_____
_____
_____
_____
_____
_____
_____
_____
_____

OPPORTUNITIES

- ☐ _____
- ☐ _____
- ☐ _____
- ☐ _____
- ☐ _____
- ☐ _____
- ☐ _____
- ☐ _____
- ☐ _____
- ☐ _____

SUNDAY	MONDAY	TUESDAY

NOTES:

Focus Verse: "Keep this Book of the Law always on your lips; meditate on it day and night, so that you may be careful to do everything written in it. Then you will be prosperous and successful." Joshua 1:8

How does this verse apply to my internal world?

_____

WEDNESDAY	THURSDAY	FRIDAY	SATURDAY

"Every choice is attached to or comes from one of your layers." p. 62

WEEK OF _____ TO _____

Areas of my Life Wheel on my radar

_____

_____

_____

_____

SUNDAY

9AM_____

_____

10AM_____

_____

11AM_____

_____

12PM_____

_____

1PM_____

_____

2PM_____

_____

3PM_____

_____

4PM_____

_____

5PM_____

_____

6PM_____

_____

MONDAY

5AM_____

_____

6AM_____

_____

7AM_____

_____

8AM_____

_____

9AM_____

_____

10AM_____

_____

11AM_____

_____

12PM_____

_____

1PM_____

_____

2PM_____

_____

3PM_____

_____

4PM_____

_____

5PM_____

_____

6PM_____

_____

7PM_____

_____

8PM_____

_____

TUESDAY

5AM_____

_____

6AM_____

_____

7AM_____

_____

8AM_____

_____

9AM_____

_____

10AM_____

_____

11AM_____

_____

12PM_____

_____

1PM_____

_____

2PM_____

_____

3PM_____

_____

4PM_____

_____

5PM_____

_____

6PM_____

_____

7PM_____

_____

8PM_____

_____

WEDNESDAY

5AM_____

_____

6AM_____

_____

7AM_____

_____

8AM_____

_____

9AM_____

_____

10AM_____

_____

11AM_____

_____

12PM_____

_____

1PM_____

_____

2PM_____

_____

3PM_____

_____

4PM_____

_____

5PM_____

_____

6PM_____

_____

7PM_____

_____

8PM_____

_____

THURSDAY	FRIDAY	SATURDAY
5AM_____	5AM_____	9AM_____
6AM_____	6AM_____	10AM_____
7AM_____	7AM_____	11AM_____
8AM_____	8AM_____	12PM_____
9AM_____	9AM_____	1PM_____
10AM_____	10AM_____	2PM_____
11AM_____	11AM_____	3PM_____
12PM_____	12PM_____	4PM_____
1PM_____	1PM_____	5PM_____
2PM_____	2PM_____	6PM_____
3PM_____	3PM_____	
4PM_____	4PM_____	
5PM_____	5PM_____	"Your choice, clarity, and commitment to forward movement is dependent on you translating your discoveries into action." p. 23
6PM_____	6PM_____	
7PM_____	7PM_____	
8PM_____	8PM_____	

Goals

_____
_____
_____
_____
_____
_____
_____

Action Steps

_____
_____
_____
_____
_____
_____
_____

Areas of my Life Wheel on my radar

_____

_____

_____

_____

MONDAY	TUESDAY	WEDNESDAY
5AM_____	5AM_____	5AM_____
6AM_____	6AM_____	6AM_____
7AM_____	7AM_____	7AM_____
8AM_____	8AM_____	8AM_____
9AM_____	9AM_____	9AM_____
10AM_____	10AM_____	10AM_____
11AM_____	11AM_____	11AM_____
12PM_____	12PM_____	12PM_____
1PM_____	1PM_____	1PM_____
2PM_____	2PM_____	2PM_____
3PM_____	3PM_____	3PM_____
4PM_____	4PM_____	4PM_____
5PM_____	5PM_____	5PM_____
6PM_____	6PM_____	6PM_____
7PM_____	7PM_____	7PM_____
8PM_____	8PM_____	8PM_____

SUNDAY

9AM_____

10AM_____

11AM_____

12PM_____

1PM_____

2PM_____

3PM_____

4PM_____

5PM_____

6PM_____

THURSDAY	FRIDAY	SATURDAY
5AM_____	5AM_____	9AM_____
6AM_____	6AM_____	10AM_____
7AM_____	7AM_____	11AM_____
8AM_____	8AM_____	12PM_____
9AM_____	9AM_____	1PM_____
10AM_____	10AM_____	2PM_____
11AM_____	11AM_____	3PM_____
12PM_____	12PM_____	4PM_____
1PM_____	1PM_____	5PM_____
2PM_____	2PM_____	6PM_____
3PM_____	3PM_____	
4PM_____	4PM_____	
5PM_____	5PM_____	
6PM_____	6PM_____	"I choose to be wise when revealing my layers to others." p. 60
7PM_____	7PM_____	
8PM_____	8PM_____	

Goals

_____
_____
_____
_____
_____
_____
_____

Action Steps

_____
_____
_____
_____
_____
_____
_____

WEEK OF _____ TO _____

Areas of my Life Wheel on my radar	MONDAY	TUESDAY	WEDNESDAY
_____	5AM_____	5AM_____	5AM_____
_____	6AM_____	6AM_____	6AM_____
_____	7AM_____	7AM_____	7AM_____
_____	8AM_____	8AM_____	8AM_____
	9AM_____	9AM_____	9AM_____

SUNDAY			
9AM_____	10AM_____	10AM_____	10AM_____
10AM_____	11AM_____	11AM_____	11AM_____
11AM_____	12PM_____	12PM_____	12PM_____
12PM_____	1PM_____	1PM_____	1PM_____
1PM_____	2PM_____	2PM_____	2PM_____
2PM_____	3PM_____	3PM_____	3PM_____
3PM_____	4PM_____	4PM_____	4PM_____
4PM_____	5PM_____	5PM_____	5PM_____
5PM_____	6PM_____	6PM_____	6PM_____
6PM_____	7PM_____	7PM_____	7PM_____
	8PM_____	8PM_____	8PM_____

THURSDAY	FRIDAY	SATURDAY
5AM	5AM	9AM
6AM	6AM	10AM
7AM	7AM	11AM
8AM	8AM	12PM
9AM	9AM	1PM
10AM	10AM	2PM
11AM	11AM	3PM
12PM	12PM	4PM
1PM	1PM	5PM
2PM	2PM	6PM
3PM	3PM	
4PM	4PM	
5PM	5PM	
6PM	6PM	"I choose to understand that my history has multiple perspectives." p. 60
7PM	7PM	
8PM	8PM	

Goals

Action Steps

WEEK OF _____ TO _____

Areas of my Life
Wheel on my radar

_____

_____

_____

_____

SUNDAY

9AM_____
_____
10AM_____
_____
11AM_____
_____
12PM_____
_____
1PM_____
_____
2PM_____
_____
3PM_____
_____
4PM_____
_____
5PM_____
_____
6PM_____
_____

MONDAY

5AM_____
_____
6AM_____
_____
7AM_____
_____
8AM_____
_____
9AM_____
_____
10AM_____
_____
11AM_____
_____
12PM_____
_____
1PM_____
_____
2PM_____
_____
3PM_____
_____
4PM_____
_____
5PM_____
_____
6PM_____
_____
7PM_____
_____
8PM_____
_____

TUESDAY

5AM_____
_____
6AM_____
_____
7AM_____
_____
8AM_____
_____
9AM_____
_____
10AM_____
_____
11AM_____
_____
12PM_____
_____
1PM_____
_____
2PM_____
_____
3PM_____
_____
4PM_____
_____
5PM_____
_____
6PM_____
_____
7PM_____
_____
8PM_____
_____

WEDNESDAY

5AM_____
_____
6AM_____
_____
7AM_____
_____
8AM_____
_____
9AM_____
_____
10AM_____
_____
11AM_____
_____
12PM_____
_____
1PM_____
_____
2PM_____
_____
3PM_____
_____
4PM_____
_____
5PM_____
_____
6PM_____
_____
7PM_____
_____
8PM_____
_____

THURSDAY	FRIDAY	SATURDAY
5AM _____	5AM _____	9AM _____
6AM _____	6AM _____	10AM _____
7AM _____	7AM _____	11AM _____
8AM _____	8AM _____	12PM _____
9AM _____	9AM _____	1PM _____
10AM _____	10AM _____	2PM _____
11AM _____	11AM _____	3PM _____
12PM _____	12PM _____	4PM _____
1PM _____	1PM _____	5PM _____
2PM _____	2PM _____	6PM _____
3PM _____	3PM _____	
4PM _____	4PM _____	
5PM _____	5PM _____	
6PM _____	6PM _____	"I choose to organize my life to achieve the life I want to have lived." p. 60
7PM _____	7PM _____	
8PM _____	8PM _____	

Goals

_____
_____
_____
_____
_____
_____
_____

Action Steps

_____
_____
_____
_____
_____
_____
_____
_____

WEEK OF _____ TO _____

Areas of my Life Wheel on my radar

_____

_____

_____

_____

SUNDAY

9AM_____

10AM_____

11AM_____

12PM_____

1PM_____

2PM_____

3PM_____

4PM_____

5PM_____

6PM_____

MONDAY

5AM_____

6AM_____

7AM_____

8AM_____

9AM_____

10AM_____

11AM_____

12PM_____

1PM_____

2PM_____

3PM_____

4PM_____

5PM_____

6PM_____

7PM_____

8PM_____

TUESDAY

5AM_____

6AM_____

7AM_____

8AM_____

9AM_____

10AM_____

11AM_____

12PM_____

1PM_____

2PM_____

3PM_____

4PM_____

5PM_____

6PM_____

7PM_____

8PM_____

WEDNESDAY

5AM_____

6AM_____

7AM_____

8AM_____

9AM_____

10AM_____

11AM_____

12PM_____

1PM_____

2PM_____

3PM_____

4PM_____

5PM_____

6PM_____

7PM_____

8PM_____

THURSDAY	FRIDAY	SATURDAY
5AM_____	5AM_____	9AM_____
_____	_____	_____
6AM_____	6AM_____	10AM_____
_____	_____	_____
7AM_____	7AM_____	11AM_____
_____	_____	_____
8AM_____	8AM_____	12PM_____
_____	_____	_____
9AM_____	9AM_____	1PM_____
_____	_____	_____
10AM_____	10AM_____	2PM_____
_____	_____	_____
11AM_____	11AM_____	3PM_____
_____	_____	_____
12PM_____	12PM_____	4PM_____
_____	_____	_____
1PM_____	1PM_____	5PM_____
_____	_____	_____
2PM_____	2PM_____	6PM_____
_____	_____	_____
3PM_____	3PM_____	
_____	_____	
4PM_____	4PM_____	
_____	_____	
5PM_____	5PM_____	
_____	_____	"Nudging you to ask yourself hard questions gives you the opportunity to determine what your new life looks like." p. 17
6PM_____	6PM_____	
_____	_____	
7PM_____	7PM_____	
_____	_____	
8PM_____	8PM_____	
_____	_____	

Goals

_____
_____
_____
_____
_____
_____
_____

Action Steps

_____
_____
_____
_____
_____
_____

NOTES_____

REJOICE!

Encourage yourself in your personal and professional life by taking advantage of opportunities to notice and celebrate accomplishments and milestones.

Successes

_____

_____

_____

_____

_____

_____

_____

Completions

_____

_____

_____

_____

_____

_____

_____

Special Events

_____

_____

_____

_____

_____

_____

_____

Memories

_____

_____

_____

_____

_____

_____

_____

MONTHLY SELF-REFLECTION:
Measuring the Net Value of Our Choices

What did you discover about yourself from the previous Life Wheel exercise? In what ways did that discovery surprise you? What specific awareness or revelations are most valuable to you?

_____
_____
_____
_____

Which area(s) did you focus on last month? Why?

_____
_____
_____
_____

How were your action steps effective or ineffective? What will you add, alter, or remove about those action steps going forward?

_____
_____
_____
_____

In what ways did having this awareness improve your personal life? Your professional life? The way you lead others?

_____
_____
_____
_____

Knowing we all fall short and have moments we don't achieve our goals and expectations, how will you extend grace to yourself to move forward?

_____
_____
_____
_____

Monthly Life Wheel Exercise

* Feel free to change or add an area. If it's important to you, it's important.

On a scale of one to ten, one being the lowest of the low and ten being best, rate your level of fulfillment in each category and record on the Life Wheel.

Business Calling _____   Financial Health _____

Physical Wellness _____   Relational Health _____

Intimacy _____   Personal Development _____

Play Time/Fun _____   Spiritual Wellness _____

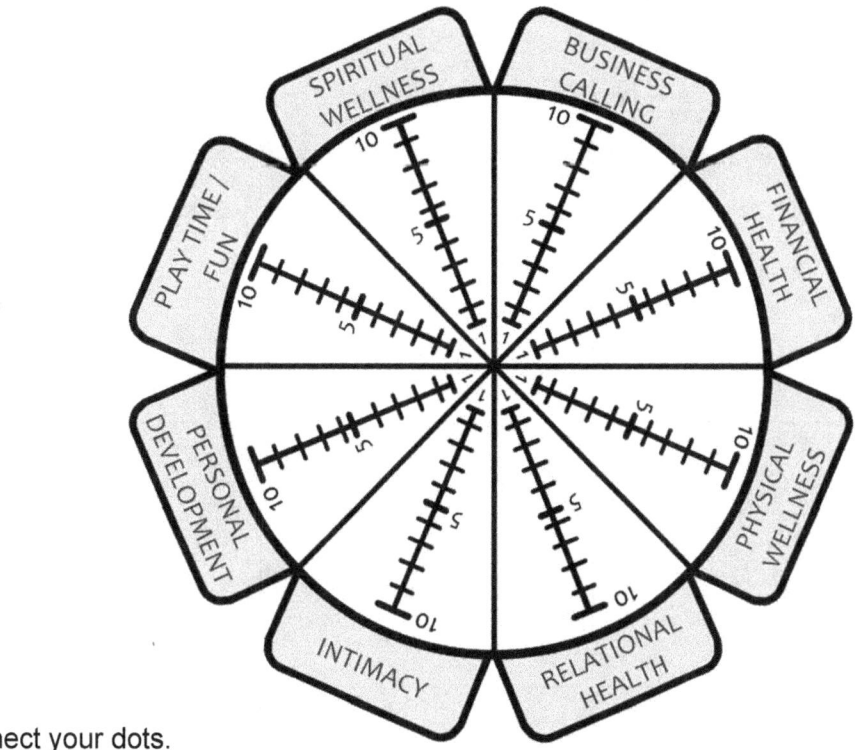

Now:

Connect your dots.

Determine what's on your radar.

What action steps can you take for improvement?

Record your action steps on your month overview. Reassess your steps each week and update accordingly using the central question: In this moment, what choice can I make and what action can I take to create the greatest net value?

Life Wheel Focus Area: *Physical Wellness: External Perspective*

What about this area is important to me?

_____

_____

MONTH: _____ YEAR: _____

Action Steps

_____
_____
_____
_____
_____
_____
_____
_____
_____
_____

OPPORTUNITIES

- [ ] _____
- [ ] _____
- [ ] _____
- [ ] _____
- [ ] _____
- [ ] _____
- [ ] _____
- [ ] _____
- [ ] _____
- [ ] _____

SUNDAY	MONDAY	TUESDAY

NOTES:

Focus Verse: "But whoever is united with the Lord is one with him in spirit."
I Corinthians 6:17

How does this verse apply to my external world?

_____

WEDNESDAY	THURSDAY	FRIDAY	SATURDAY

"Our beliefs are the foundation of our thoughts, which become words
we say internally to ourselves and aloud to others." p. 68

WEEK OF _____ TO _____

Areas of my Life Wheel on my radar

_____

_____

_____

_____

MONDAY

5AM_____

_____

6AM_____

_____

7AM_____

_____

8AM_____

_____

9AM_____

_____

10AM_____

_____

11AM_____

_____

12PM_____

_____

1PM_____

_____

2PM_____

_____

3PM_____

_____

4PM_____

_____

5PM_____

_____

6PM_____

_____

7PM_____

_____

8PM_____

_____

TUESDAY

5AM_____

_____

6AM_____

_____

7AM_____

_____

8AM_____

_____

9AM_____

_____

10AM_____

_____

11AM_____

_____

12PM_____

_____

1PM_____

_____

2PM_____

_____

3PM_____

_____

4PM_____

_____

5PM_____

_____

6PM_____

_____

7PM_____

_____

8PM_____

_____

WEDNESDAY

5AM_____

_____

6AM_____

_____

7AM_____

_____

8AM_____

_____

9AM_____

_____

10AM_____

_____

11AM_____

_____

12PM_____

_____

1PM_____

_____

2PM_____

_____

3PM_____

_____

4PM_____

_____

5PM_____

_____

6PM_____

_____

7PM_____

_____

8PM_____

_____

SUNDAY

9AM_____

_____

10AM_____

_____

11AM_____

_____

12PM_____

_____

1PM_____

_____

2PM_____

_____

3PM_____

_____

4PM_____

_____

5PM_____

_____

6PM_____

_____

THURSDAY	FRIDAY	SATURDAY
5AM_____	5AM_____	9AM_____
6AM_____	6AM_____	10AM_____
7AM_____	7AM_____	11AM_____
8AM_____	8AM_____	12PM_____
9AM_____	9AM_____	1PM_____
10AM_____	10AM_____	2PM_____
11AM_____	11AM_____	3PM_____
12PM_____	12PM_____	4PM_____
1PM_____	1PM_____	5PM_____
2PM_____	2PM_____	6PM_____
3PM_____	3PM_____	
4PM_____	4PM_____	
5PM_____	5PM_____	"I choose to experience *being*." P. 105
6PM_____	6PM_____	
7PM_____	7PM_____	
8PM_____	8PM_____	

Goals

_____
_____
_____
_____
_____
_____
_____

Action Steps

_____
_____
_____
_____
_____
_____
_____

WEEK OF _____ TO _____

Areas of my Life Wheel on my radar	MONDAY	TUESDAY	WEDNESDAY
_____	5AM_____	5AM_____	5AM_____
_____	6AM_____	6AM_____	6AM_____
_____	7AM_____	7AM_____	7AM_____
_____	8AM_____	8AM_____	8AM_____
	9AM_____	9AM_____	9AM_____

SUNDAY	MONDAY	TUESDAY	WEDNESDAY
9AM_____	10AM_____	10AM_____	10AM_____
10AM_____	11AM_____	11AM_____	11AM_____
11AM_____	12PM_____	12PM_____	12PM_____
12PM_____	1PM_____	1PM_____	1PM_____
1PM_____	2PM_____	2PM_____	2PM_____
2PM_____	3PM_____	3PM_____	3PM_____
3PM_____	4PM_____	4PM_____	4PM_____
4PM_____	5PM_____	5PM_____	5PM_____
5PM_____	6PM_____	6PM_____	6PM_____
6PM_____	7PM_____	7PM_____	7PM_____
	8PM_____	8PM_____	8PM_____

THURSDAY	FRIDAY	SATURDAY
5AM_____	5AM_____	9AM_____
6AM_____	6AM_____	10AM_____
7AM_____	7AM_____	11AM_____
8AM_____	8AM_____	12PM_____
9AM_____	9AM_____	1PM_____
10AM_____	10AM_____	2PM_____
11AM_____	11AM_____	3PM_____
12PM_____	12PM_____	4PM_____
1PM_____	1PM_____	5PM_____
2PM_____	2PM_____	6PM_____
3PM_____	3PM_____	
4PM_____	4PM_____	
5PM_____	5PM_____	"When we take the time to discover how others will invite us into their layers and meet them where they are, we show initiative and how much we value them." p. 116
6PM_____	6PM_____	
7PM_____	7PM_____	
8PM_____	8PM_____	

Goals

_____
_____
_____
_____
_____
_____
_____

Action Steps

_____
_____
_____
_____
_____
_____
_____

WEEK OF _____ TO _____

Areas of my Life Wheel on my radar

_____

_____

_____

_____

SUNDAY	MONDAY	TUESDAY	WEDNESDAY
9AM_____	5AM_____	5AM_____	5AM_____
10AM_____	6AM_____	6AM_____	6AM_____
11AM_____	7AM_____	7AM_____	7AM_____
12PM_____	8AM_____	8AM_____	8AM_____
1PM_____	9AM_____	9AM_____	9AM_____
2PM_____	10AM_____	10AM_____	10AM_____
3PM_____	11AM_____	11AM_____	11AM_____
4PM_____	12PM_____	12PM_____	12PM_____
5PM_____	1PM_____	1PM_____	1PM_____
6PM_____	2PM_____	2PM_____	2PM_____
	3PM_____	3PM_____	3PM_____
	4PM_____	4PM_____	4PM_____
	5PM_____	5PM_____	5PM_____
	6PM_____	6PM_____	6PM_____
	7PM_____	7PM_____	7PM_____
	8PM_____	8PM_____	8PM_____

THURSDAY	FRIDAY	SATURDAY
5AM_____	5AM_____	9AM_____
6AM_____	6AM_____	10AM_____
7AM_____	7AM_____	11AM_____
8AM_____	8AM_____	12PM_____
9AM_____	9AM_____	1PM_____
10AM_____	10AM_____	2PM_____
11AM_____	11AM_____	3PM_____
12PM_____	12PM_____	4PM_____
1PM_____	1PM_____	5PM_____
2PM_____	2PM_____	6PM_____
3PM_____	3PM_____	
4PM_____	4PM_____	
5PM_____	5PM_____	"We get to choose how we manage our responsibilities, yet because of the reciprocal nature of accountability and responsibility, mismanaging one will negatively affect the other." p.126
6PM_____	6PM_____	
7PM_____	7PM_____	
8PM_____	8PM_____	

Goals

_____
_____
_____
_____
_____
_____
_____

Action Steps

_____
_____
_____
_____
_____
_____
_____

WEEK OF _____ TO _____

Areas of my Life
Wheel on my radar

_____

_____

_____

_____

SUNDAY	MONDAY	TUESDAY	WEDNESDAY
	5AM_____	5AM_____	5AM_____
	6AM_____	6AM_____	6AM_____
	7AM_____	7AM_____	7AM_____
	8AM_____	8AM_____	8AM_____
9AM_____	9AM_____	9AM_____	9AM_____
10AM_____	10AM_____	10AM_____	10AM_____
11AM_____	11AM_____	11AM_____	11AM_____
12PM_____	12PM_____	12PM_____	12PM_____
1PM_____	1PM_____	1PM_____	1PM_____
2PM_____	2PM_____	2PM_____	2PM_____
3PM_____	3PM_____	3PM_____	3PM_____
4PM_____	4PM_____	4PM_____	4PM_____
5PM_____	5PM_____	5PM_____	5PM_____
6PM_____	6PM_____	6PM_____	6PM_____
	7PM_____	7PM_____	7PM_____
	8PM_____	8PM_____	8PM_____

THURSDAY	FRIDAY	SATURDAY
5AM_____	5AM_____	9AM_____
6AM_____	6AM_____	10AM_____
7AM_____	7AM_____	11AM_____
8AM_____	8AM_____	12PM_____
9AM_____	9AM_____	1PM_____
10AM_____	10AM_____	2PM_____
11AM_____	11AM_____	3PM_____
12PM_____	12PM_____	4PM_____
1PM_____	1PM_____	5PM_____
2PM_____	2PM_____	6PM_____
3PM_____	3PM_____	
4PM_____	4PM_____	
5PM_____	5PM_____	"We have the power to tear down the walls we've built and step out of our respective jail cells." p. 8
6PM_____	6PM_____	
7PM_____	7PM_____	
8PM_____	8PM_____	

Goals

_____
_____
_____
_____
_____
_____
_____

Action Steps

_____
_____
_____
_____
_____
_____
_____

WEEK OF _____ TO _____

Areas of my Life Wheel on my radar

_____

_____

_____

_____

SUNDAY

9AM_____
_____
10AM_____
_____
11AM_____
_____
12PM_____
_____
1PM_____
_____
2PM_____
_____
3PM_____
_____
4PM_____
_____
5PM_____
_____
6PM_____
_____

MONDAY

5AM_____
_____
6AM_____
_____
7AM_____
_____
8AM_____
_____
9AM_____
_____
10AM_____
_____
11AM_____
_____
12PM_____
_____
1PM_____
_____
2PM_____
_____
3PM_____
_____
4PM_____
_____
5PM_____
_____
6PM_____
_____
7PM_____
_____
8PM_____
_____

TUESDAY

5AM_____
_____
6AM_____
_____
7AM_____
_____
8AM_____
_____
9AM_____
_____
10AM_____
_____
11AM_____
_____
12PM_____
_____
1PM_____
_____
2PM_____
_____
3PM_____
_____
4PM_____
_____
5PM_____
_____
6PM_____
_____
7PM_____
_____
8PM_____
_____

WEDNESDAY

5AM_____
_____
6AM_____
_____
7AM_____
_____
8AM_____
_____
9AM_____
_____
10AM_____
_____
11AM_____
_____
12PM_____
_____
1PM_____
_____
2PM_____
_____
3PM_____
_____
4PM_____
_____
5PM_____
_____
6PM_____
_____
7PM_____
_____
8PM_____
_____

THURSDAY	FRIDAY	SATURDAY
5AM_____	5AM_____	9AM_____
6AM_____	6AM_____	10AM_____
7AM_____	7AM_____	11AM_____
8AM_____	8AM_____	12PM_____
9AM_____	9AM_____	1PM_____
10AM_____	10AM_____	2PM_____
11AM_____	11AM_____	3PM_____
12PM_____	12PM_____	4PM_____
1PM_____	1PM_____	5PM_____
2PM_____	2PM_____	6PM_____
3PM_____	3PM_____	
4PM_____	4PM_____	
5PM_____	5PM_____	"Every choice we make has a domino effect in our lives and the lives of others." p. 42
6PM_____	6PM_____	
7PM_____	7PM_____	
8PM_____	8PM_____	

Goals

_____
_____
_____
_____
_____
_____
_____

Action Steps

_____
_____
_____
_____
_____
_____

NOTES_____

NOTES_____

MONTHLY SELF-REFLECTION:
Measuring the Net Value of Our Choices

What did you discover about yourself from the previous Life Wheel exercise? In what ways did that discovery surprise you? What specific awareness or revelations are most valuable to you?

_____
_____
_____
_____

Which area(s) did you focus on last month? Why?

_____
_____
_____
_____

How were your action steps effective or ineffective? What will you add, alter, or remove about those action steps going forward?

_____
_____
_____
_____

In what ways did having this awareness improve your personal life? Your professional life? The way you lead others?

_____
_____
_____
_____

Knowing we all fall short and have moments we don't achieve our goals and expectations, how will you extend grace to yourself to move forward?

_____
_____
_____
_____

Monthly Life Wheel Exercise

* Feel free to change or add an area. If it's important to you, it's important.

On a scale of one to ten, one being the lowest of the low and ten being best, rate your level of fulfillment in each category and record on the Life Wheel.

Business Calling _____   Financial Health _____

Physical Wellness _____   Relational Health _____

Intimacy _____   Personal Development _____

Play Time/Fun _____   Spiritual Wellness _____

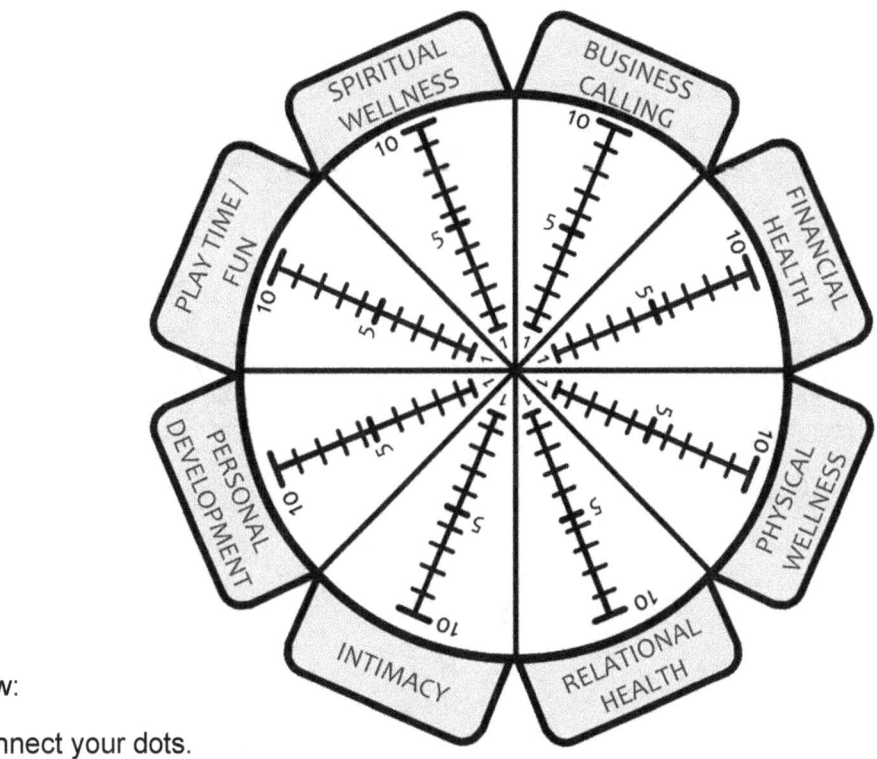

Now:

Connect your dots.

Determine what's on your radar.

What action steps can you take for improvement?

Record your action steps on your month overview. Reassess your steps each week and update accordingly using the central question: In this moment, what choice can I make and what action can I take to create the greatest net value?

Life Wheel Focus Area: *Physical Wellness: Internal Perspective*
What about this area is important to me?

_____

_____

MONTH: _____   YEAR: _____

Action Steps
_____
_____
_____
_____
_____
_____
_____
_____
_____

OPPORTUNITIES
- [ ] _____
- [ ] _____
- [ ] _____
- [ ] _____
- [ ] _____
- [ ] _____
- [ ] _____
- [ ] _____
- [ ] _____
- [ ] _____

SUNDAY	MONDAY	TUESDAY

NOTES:

Focus Verse: "For the kingdom of God is not a matter of eating and drinking, but of righteousness, peace and joy in the Holy Spirit," Romans 14:17

How does this verse apply to my internal world?

_____

WEDNESDAY	THURSDAY	FRIDAY	SATURDAY

"I choose to consider my thinking patterns." p.105

WEEK OF _____ TO _____

Areas of my Life Wheel on my radar

_____

_____

_____

_____

SUNDAY	MONDAY	TUESDAY	WEDNESDAY
9AM_____	5AM_____	5AM_____	5AM_____
_____	_____	_____	_____
10AM_____	6AM_____	6AM_____	6AM_____
_____	_____	_____	_____
11AM_____	7AM_____	7AM_____	7AM_____
_____	_____	_____	_____
12PM_____	8AM_____	8AM_____	8AM_____
_____	_____	_____	_____
1PM_____	9AM_____	9AM_____	9AM_____
_____	_____	_____	_____
2PM_____	10AM_____	10AM_____	10AM_____
_____	_____	_____	_____
3PM_____	11AM_____	11AM_____	11AM_____
_____	_____	_____	_____
4PM_____	12PM_____	12PM_____	12PM_____
_____	_____	_____	_____
5PM_____	1PM_____	1PM_____	1PM_____
_____	_____	_____	_____
6PM_____	2PM_____	2PM_____	2PM_____
_____	_____	_____	_____
	3PM_____	3PM_____	3PM_____
	_____	_____	_____
	4PM_____	4PM_____	4PM_____
	_____	_____	_____
	5PM_____	5PM_____	5PM_____
	_____	_____	_____
	6PM_____	6PM_____	6PM_____
	_____	_____	_____
	7PM_____	7PM_____	7PM_____
	_____	_____	_____
	8PM_____	8PM_____	8PM_____
	_____	_____	_____

THURSDAY	FRIDAY	SATURDAY
5AM_____	5AM_____	9AM_____
_____	_____	_____
6AM_____	6AM_____	10AM_____
_____	_____	_____
7AM_____	7AM_____	11AM_____
_____	_____	_____
8AM_____	8AM_____	12PM_____
_____	_____	_____
9AM_____	9AM_____	1PM_____
_____	_____	_____
10AM_____	10AM_____	2PM_____
_____	_____	_____
11AM_____	11AM_____	3PM_____
_____	_____	_____
12PM_____	12PM_____	4PM_____
_____	_____	_____
1PM_____	1PM_____	5PM_____
_____	_____	_____
2PM_____	2PM_____	6PM_____
_____	_____	_____
3PM_____	3PM_____	
_____	_____	
4PM_____	4PM_____	
_____	_____	
5PM_____	5PM_____	
_____	_____	
6PM_____	6PM_____	"I choose to unveil one layer at a time." p.160
_____	_____	
7PM_____	7PM_____	
_____	_____	
8PM_____	8PM_____	
_____	_____	

Goals

_____
_____
_____
_____
_____
_____

Action Steps

_____
_____
_____
_____
_____
_____

WEEK OF _____ TO _____

Areas of my Life
Wheel on my radar

_____

_____

_____

_____

SUNDAY	MONDAY	TUESDAY	WEDNESDAY
9AM_____	5AM_____	5AM_____	5AM_____
10AM_____	6AM_____	6AM_____	6AM_____
11AM_____	7AM_____	7AM_____	7AM_____
12PM_____	8AM_____	8AM_____	8AM_____
1PM_____	9AM_____	9AM_____	9AM_____
2PM_____	10AM_____	10AM_____	10AM_____
3PM_____	11AM_____	11AM_____	11AM_____
4PM_____	12PM_____	12PM_____	12PM_____
5PM_____	1PM_____	1PM_____	1PM_____
6PM_____	2PM_____	2PM_____	2PM_____
	3PM_____	3PM_____	3PM_____
	4PM_____	4PM_____	4PM_____
	5PM_____	5PM_____	5PM_____
	6PM_____	6PM_____	6PM_____
	7PM_____	7PM_____	7PM_____
	8PM_____	8PM_____	8PM_____

THURSDAY	FRIDAY	SATURDAY
5AM_____	5AM_____	9AM_____
6AM_____	6AM_____	10AM_____
7AM_____	7AM_____	11AM_____
8AM_____	8AM_____	12PM_____
9AM_____	9AM_____	1PM_____
10AM_____	10AM_____	2PM_____
11AM_____	11AM_____	3PM_____
12PM_____	12PM_____	4PM_____
1PM_____	1PM_____	5PM_____
2PM_____	2PM_____	6PM_____
3PM_____	3PM_____	
4PM_____	4PM_____	
5PM_____	5PM_____	
6PM_____	6PM_____	"I choose to connect with others to take my next steps."
7PM_____	7PM_____	p. 160
8PM_____	8PM_____	

Goals

_____
_____
_____
_____
_____
_____
_____

Action Steps

_____
_____
_____
_____
_____
_____

WEEK OF _____ TO _____

Areas of my Life Wheel on my radar

_____

_____

_____

_____

MONDAY	TUESDAY	WEDNESDAY
5AM_____	5AM_____	5AM_____
6AM_____	6AM_____	6AM_____
7AM_____	7AM_____	7AM_____
8AM_____	8AM_____	8AM_____
9AM_____	9AM_____	9AM_____
10AM_____	10AM_____	10AM_____
11AM_____	11AM_____	11AM_____
12PM_____	12PM_____	12PM_____
1PM_____	1PM_____	1PM_____
2PM_____	2PM_____	2PM_____
3PM_____	3PM_____	3PM_____
4PM_____	4PM_____	4PM_____
5PM_____	5PM_____	5PM_____
6PM_____	6PM_____	6PM_____
7PM_____	7PM_____	7PM_____
8PM_____	8PM_____	8PM_____

SUNDAY

9AM_____

10AM_____

11AM_____

12PM_____

1PM_____

2PM_____

3PM_____

4PM_____

5PM_____

6PM_____

THURSDAY	FRIDAY	SATURDAY
5AM_____	5AM_____	9AM_____
6AM_____	6AM_____	10AM_____
7AM_____	7AM_____	11AM_____
8AM_____	8AM_____	12PM_____
9AM_____	9AM_____	1PM_____
10AM_____	10AM_____	2PM_____
11AM_____	11AM_____	3PM_____
12PM_____	12PM_____	4PM_____
1PM_____	1PM_____	5PM_____
2PM_____	2PM_____	6PM_____
3PM_____	3PM_____	
4PM_____	4PM_____	
5PM_____	5PM_____	
6PM_____	6PM_____	"I choose to be an Onion Slayer for life." p.160
7PM_____	7PM_____	
8PM_____	8PM_____	

Goals

_____
_____
_____
_____
_____
_____
_____

Action Steps

_____
_____
_____
_____
_____
_____
_____

WEEK OF _____ TO _____

Areas of my Life Wheel on my radar

_____

_____

_____

_____

MONDAY	TUESDAY	WEDNESDAY
5AM_____	5AM_____	5AM_____
6AM_____	6AM_____	6AM_____
7AM_____	7AM_____	7AM_____
8AM_____	8AM_____	8AM_____
9AM_____	9AM_____	9AM_____
10AM_____	10AM_____	10AM_____
11AM_____	11AM_____	11AM_____
12PM_____	12PM_____	12PM_____
1PM_____	1PM_____	1PM_____
2PM_____	2PM_____	2PM_____
3PM_____	3PM_____	3PM_____
4PM_____	4PM_____	4PM_____
5PM_____	5PM_____	5PM_____
6PM_____	6PM_____	6PM_____
7PM_____	7PM_____	7PM_____
8PM_____	8PM_____	8PM_____

SUNDAY

9AM_____

10AM_____

11AM_____

12PM_____

1PM_____

2PM_____

3PM_____

4PM_____

5PM_____

6PM_____

THURSDAY	FRIDAY	SATURDAY
5AM_____	5AM_____	9AM_____
6AM_____	6AM_____	10AM_____
7AM_____	7AM_____	11AM_____
8AM_____	8AM_____	12PM_____
9AM_____	9AM_____	1PM_____
10AM_____	10AM_____	2PM_____
11AM_____	11AM_____	3PM_____
12PM_____	12PM_____	4PM_____
1PM_____	1PM_____	5PM_____
2PM_____	2PM_____	6PM_____
3PM_____	3PM_____	
4PM_____	4PM_____	
5PM_____	5PM_____	"We hold the key to releasing the light within us and being a light to others." p.8
6PM_____	6PM_____	
7PM_____	7PM_____	
8PM_____	8PM_____	

Goals

_____
_____
_____
_____
_____
_____

Action Steps

_____
_____
_____
_____
_____
_____
_____

WEEK OF _____ TO _____

Areas of my Life Wheel on my radar

_____

_____

_____

_____

SUNDAY

9AM_____
_____
10AM_____
_____
11AM_____
_____
12PM_____
_____
1PM_____
_____
2PM_____
_____
3PM_____
_____
4PM_____
_____
5PM_____
_____
6PM_____
_____

MONDAY

5AM_____
_____
6AM_____
_____
7AM_____
_____
8AM_____
_____
9AM_____
_____
10AM_____
_____
11AM_____
_____
12PM_____
_____
1PM_____
_____
2PM_____
_____
3PM_____
_____
4PM_____
_____
5PM_____
_____
6PM_____
_____
7PM_____
_____
8PM_____
_____

TUESDAY

5AM_____
_____
6AM_____
_____
7AM_____
_____
8AM_____
_____
9AM_____
_____
10AM_____
_____
11AM_____
_____
12PM_____
_____
1PM_____
_____
2PM_____
_____
3PM_____
_____
4PM_____
_____
5PM_____
_____
6PM_____
_____
7PM_____
_____
8PM_____
_____

WEDNESDAY

5AM_____
_____
6AM_____
_____
7AM_____
_____
8AM_____
_____
9AM_____
_____
10AM_____
_____
11AM_____
_____
12PM_____
_____
1PM_____
_____
2PM_____
_____
3PM_____
_____
4PM_____
_____
5PM_____
_____
6PM_____
_____
7PM_____
_____
8PM_____
_____

THURSDAY	FRIDAY	SATURDAY
5AM_____	5AM_____	9AM_____
6AM_____	6AM_____	10AM_____
7AM_____	7AM_____	11AM_____
8AM_____	8AM_____	12PM_____
9AM_____	9AM_____	1PM_____
10AM_____	10AM_____	2PM_____
11AM_____	11AM_____	3PM_____
12PM_____	12PM_____	4PM_____
1PM_____	1PM_____	5PM_____
2PM_____	2PM_____	6PM_____
3PM_____	3PM_____	
4PM_____	4PM_____	
5PM_____	5PM_____	"Sometimes our perceptions and defense mechanisms create complex systems of multiple protective layers, we might be unaware of." p. 64
6PM_____	6PM_____	
7PM_____	7PM_____	
8PM_____	8PM_____	

Goals

_____
_____
_____
_____
_____
_____
_____

Action Steps

_____
_____
_____
_____
_____
_____

NOTES_____

NOTES

MONTHLY SELF-REFLECTION:
Measuring the Net Value of Our Choices

What did you discover about yourself from the previous Life Wheel exercise? In what ways did that discovery surprise you? What specific awareness or revelations are most valuable to you?

_____
_____
_____
_____

Which area(s) did you focus on last month? Why?

_____
_____
_____
_____

How were your action steps effective or ineffective? What will you add, alter, or remove about those action steps going forward?

_____
_____
_____
_____

In what ways did having this awareness improve your personal life? Your professional life? The way you lead others?

_____
_____
_____
_____

Knowing we all fall short and have moments we don't achieve our goals and expectations, how will you extend grace to yourself to move forward?

_____
_____
_____
_____

Monthly Life Wheel Exercise

* Feel free to change or add an area. If it's important to you, it's important.

On a scale of one to ten, one being the lowest of the low and ten being best, rate your level of fulfillment in each category and record on the Life Wheel.

Business Calling _____   Financial Health _____

Physical Wellness _____   Relational Health _____

Intimacy _____   Personal Development _____

Play Time/Fun _____   Spiritual Wellness _____

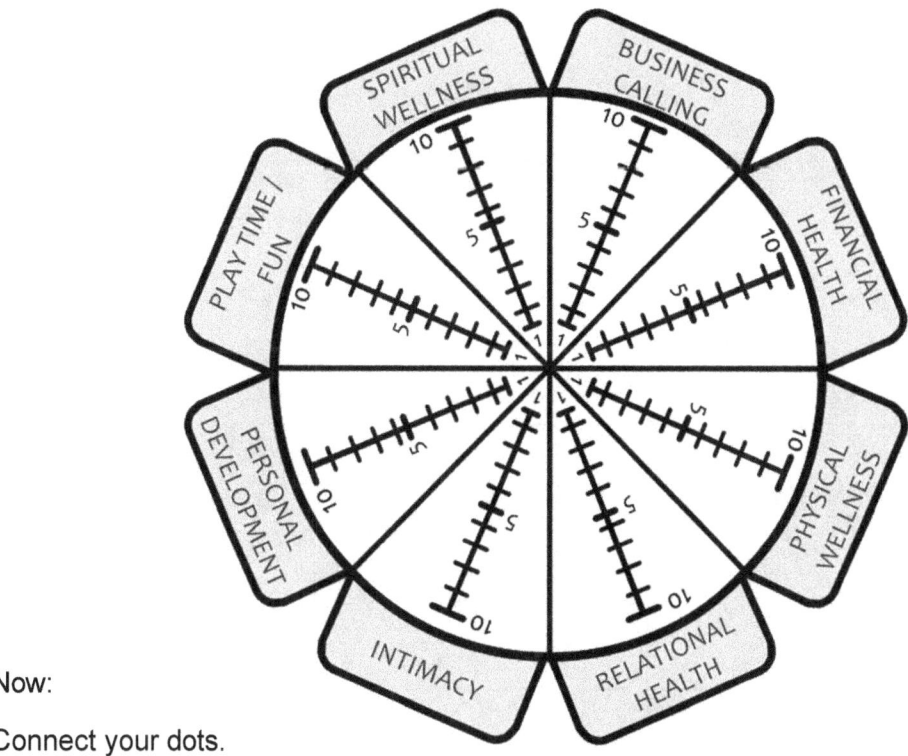

Now:

Connect your dots.

Determine what's on your radar.

What action steps can you take for improvement?

Record your action steps on your month overview. Reassess your steps each week and update accordingly using the central question: In this moment, what choice can I make and what action can I take to create the greatest net value?

Life Wheel Focus Area: *Relational Health: External Perspective*

What about this area is important to me?

_____

_____

MONTH: _____   YEAR: _____

Action Steps

_____
_____
_____
_____
_____
_____
_____
_____
_____
_____
_____

OPPORTUNITIES

- ☐ _____
- ☐ _____
- ☐ _____
- ☐ _____
- ☐ _____
- ☐ _____
- ☐ _____
- ☐ _____
- ☐ _____
- ☐ _____

SUNDAY	MONDAY	TUESDAY

NOTES:

How does this verse apply to my external world?

_____

WEDNESDAY	THURSDAY	FRIDAY	SATURDAY

"Whether we realize it or not, whether we admit it or not, each of us has beliefs about life and ourselves that appear to be true but aren't necessarily true." p. 75

WEEK OF _____ TO _____

Areas of my Life Wheel on my radar

_____

_____

_____

_____

SUNDAY

9AM_____
_____
10AM_____
_____
11AM_____
_____
12PM_____
_____
1PM_____
_____
2PM_____
_____
3PM_____
_____
4PM_____
_____
5PM_____
_____
6PM_____
_____

MONDAY

5AM_____
_____
6AM_____
_____
7AM_____
_____
8AM_____
_____
9AM_____
_____
10AM_____
_____
11AM_____
_____
12PM_____
_____
1PM_____
_____
2PM_____
_____
3PM_____
_____
4PM_____
_____
5PM_____
_____
6PM_____
_____
7PM_____
_____
8PM_____
_____

TUESDAY

5AM_____
_____
6AM_____
_____
7AM_____
_____
8AM_____
_____
9AM_____
_____
10AM_____
_____
11AM_____
_____
12PM_____
_____
1PM_____
_____
2PM_____
_____
3PM_____
_____
4PM_____
_____
5PM_____
_____
6PM_____
_____
7PM_____
_____
8PM_____
_____

WEDNESDAY

5AM_____
_____
6AM_____
_____
7AM_____
_____
8AM_____
_____
9AM_____
_____
10AM_____
_____
11AM_____
_____
12PM_____
_____
1PM_____
_____
2PM_____
_____
3PM_____
_____
4PM_____
_____
5PM_____
_____
6PM_____
_____
7PM_____
_____
8PM_____
_____

THURSDAY	FRIDAY	SATURDAY
5AM_____	5AM_____	9AM_____
6AM_____	6AM_____	10AM_____
7AM_____	7AM_____	11AM_____
8AM_____	8AM_____	12PM_____
9AM_____	9AM_____	1PM_____
10AM_____	10AM_____	2PM_____
11AM_____	11AM_____	3PM_____
12PM_____	12PM_____	4PM_____
1PM_____	1PM_____	5PM_____
2PM_____	2PM_____	6PM_____
3PM_____	3PM_____	
4PM_____	4PM_____	
5PM_____	5PM_____	
6PM_____	6PM_____	"I choose to love others with brotherly love, sometimes from a distance."
7PM_____	7PM_____	p. 60
8PM_____	8PM_____	

Goals

_____

_____

_____

_____

_____

_____

_____

Action Steps

_____

_____

_____

_____

_____

_____

_____

_____

WEEK OF _____ TO _____

Areas of my Life Wheel on my radar

_____

_____

_____

_____

MONDAY	TUESDAY	WEDNESDAY
5AM_____	5AM_____	5AM_____
6AM_____	6AM_____	6AM_____
7AM_____	7AM_____	7AM_____
8AM_____	8AM_____	8AM_____
9AM_____	9AM_____	9AM_____
10AM_____	10AM_____	10AM_____
11AM_____	11AM_____	11AM_____
12PM_____	12PM_____	12PM_____
1PM_____	1PM_____	1PM_____
2PM_____	2PM_____	2PM_____
3PM_____	3PM_____	3PM_____
4PM_____	4PM_____	4PM_____
5PM_____	5PM_____	5PM_____
6PM_____	6PM_____	6PM_____
7PM_____	7PM_____	7PM_____
8PM_____	8PM_____	8PM_____

SUNDAY

9AM_____

10AM_____

11AM_____

12PM_____

1PM_____

2PM_____

3PM_____

4PM_____

5PM_____

6PM_____

THURSDAY	FRIDAY	SATURDAY
5AM_____	5AM_____	9AM_____
6AM_____	6AM_____	10AM_____
7AM_____	7AM_____	11AM_____
8AM_____	8AM_____	12PM_____
9AM_____	9AM_____	1PM_____
10AM_____	10AM_____	2PM_____
11AM_____	11AM_____	3PM_____
12PM_____	12PM_____	4PM_____
1PM_____	1PM_____	5PM_____
2PM_____	2PM_____	6PM_____
3PM_____	3PM_____	
4PM_____	4PM_____	
5PM_____	5PM_____	
6PM_____	6PM_____	"I choose to be consciously aware of my five closest friends." p. 60
7PM_____	7PM_____	
8PM_____	8PM_____	

Goals

_____
_____
_____
_____
_____
_____
_____

Action Steps

_____
_____
_____
_____
_____
_____
_____

WEEK OF _____ TO _____

Areas of my Life Wheel on my radar

_____

_____

_____

_____

SUNDAY	MONDAY	TUESDAY	WEDNESDAY
9AM _____	5AM _____	5AM _____	5AM _____
10AM _____	6AM _____	6AM _____	6AM _____
11AM _____	7AM _____	7AM _____	7AM _____
12PM _____	8AM _____	8AM _____	8AM _____
1PM _____	9AM _____	9AM _____	9AM _____
2PM _____	10AM _____	10AM _____	10AM _____
3PM _____	11AM _____	11AM _____	11AM _____
4PM _____	12PM _____	12PM _____	12PM _____
5PM _____	1PM _____	1PM _____	1PM _____
6PM _____	2PM _____	2PM _____	2PM _____
	3PM _____	3PM _____	3PM _____
	4PM _____	4PM _____	4PM _____
	5PM _____	5PM _____	5PM _____
	6PM _____	6PM _____	6PM _____
	7PM _____	7PM _____	7PM _____
	8PM _____	8PM _____	8PM _____

THURSDAY	FRIDAY	SATURDAY
5AM_____	5AM_____	9AM_____
6AM_____	6AM_____	10AM_____
7AM_____	7AM_____	11AM_____
8AM_____	8AM_____	12PM_____
9AM_____	9AM_____	1PM_____
10AM_____	10AM_____	2PM_____
11AM_____	11AM_____	3PM_____
12PM_____	12PM_____	4PM_____
1PM_____	1PM_____	5PM_____
2PM_____	2PM_____	6PM_____
3PM_____	3PM_____	
4PM_____	4PM_____	
5PM_____	5PM_____	"I choose to see my choices are attached to my layers." p. 80
6PM_____	6PM_____	
7PM_____	7PM_____	
8PM_____	8PM_____	

Goals

_____
_____
_____
_____
_____
_____
_____

Action Steps

_____
_____
_____
_____
_____
_____
_____
_____

WEEK OF _____ TO _____

	MONDAY	TUESDAY	WEDNESDAY

Areas of my Life Wheel on my radar

_____

_____

_____

_____

MONDAY	TUESDAY	WEDNESDAY
5AM_____	5AM_____	5AM_____
6AM_____	6AM_____	6AM_____
7AM_____	7AM_____	7AM_____
8AM_____	8AM_____	8AM_____
9AM_____	9AM_____	9AM_____
10AM_____	10AM_____	10AM_____
11AM_____	11AM_____	11AM_____
12PM_____	12PM_____	12PM_____
1PM_____	1PM_____	1PM_____
2PM_____	2PM_____	2PM_____
3PM_____	3PM_____	3PM_____
4PM_____	4PM_____	4PM_____
5PM_____	5PM_____	5PM_____
6PM_____	6PM_____	6PM_____
7PM_____	7PM_____	7PM_____
8PM_____	8PM_____	8PM_____

SUNDAY

9AM_____

10AM_____

11AM_____

12PM_____

1PM_____

2PM_____

3PM_____

4PM_____

5PM_____

6PM_____

THURSDAY	FRIDAY	SATURDAY
5AM_____	5AM_____	9AM_____
_____	_____	_____
6AM_____	6AM_____	10AM_____
_____	_____	_____
7AM_____	7AM_____	11AM_____
_____	_____	_____
8AM_____	8AM_____	12PM_____
_____	_____	_____
9AM_____	9AM_____	1PM_____
_____	_____	_____
10AM_____	10AM_____	2PM_____
_____	_____	_____
11AM_____	11AM_____	3PM_____
_____	_____	_____
12PM_____	12PM_____	4PM_____
_____	_____	_____
1PM_____	1PM_____	5PM_____
_____	_____	_____
2PM_____	2PM_____	6PM_____
_____	_____	_____
3PM_____	3PM_____	
_____	_____	
4PM_____	4PM_____	
_____	_____	
5PM_____	5PM_____	"Our message, our presence, and our beliefs will attract the people who come into our lives, the ones we want and those we don't want." p. 94
_____	_____	
6PM_____	6PM_____	
_____	_____	
7PM_____	7PM_____	
_____	_____	
8PM_____	8PM_____	
_____	_____	

Goals

_____
_____
_____
_____
_____
_____
_____

Action Steps

_____
_____
_____
_____
_____
_____
_____

WEEK OF _____ TO _____

MONDAY	TUESDAY	WEDNESDAY
5AM _____	5AM _____	5AM _____
_____	_____	_____
6AM _____	6AM _____	6AM _____
_____	_____	_____
7AM _____	7AM _____	7AM _____
_____	_____	_____
8AM _____	8AM _____	8AM _____
_____	_____	_____
9AM _____	9AM _____	9AM _____
_____	_____	_____
10AM _____	10AM _____	10AM _____
_____	_____	_____
11AM _____	11AM _____	11AM _____
_____	_____	_____
12PM _____	12PM _____	12PM _____
_____	_____	_____
1PM _____	1PM _____	1PM _____
_____	_____	_____
2PM _____	2PM _____	2PM _____
_____	_____	_____
3PM _____	3PM _____	3PM _____
_____	_____	_____
4PM _____	4PM _____	4PM _____
_____	_____	_____
5PM _____	5PM _____	5PM _____
_____	_____	_____
6PM _____	6PM _____	6PM _____
_____	_____	_____
7PM _____	7PM _____	7PM _____
_____	_____	_____
8PM _____	8PM _____	8PM _____
_____	_____	_____

SUNDAY

9AM _____

_____

10AM _____

_____

11AM _____

_____

12PM _____

_____

1PM _____

_____

2PM _____

_____

3PM _____

_____

4PM _____

_____

5PM _____

_____

6PM _____

_____

THURSDAY	FRIDAY	SATURDAY
5AM_____	5AM_____	9AM_____
6AM_____	6AM_____	10AM_____
7AM_____	7AM_____	11AM_____
8AM_____	8AM_____	12PM_____
9AM_____	9AM_____	1PM_____
10AM_____	10AM_____	2PM_____
11AM_____	11AM_____	3PM_____
12PM_____	12PM_____	4PM_____
1PM_____	1PM_____	5PM_____
2PM_____	2PM_____	6PM_____
3PM_____	3PM_____	
4PM_____	4PM_____	
5PM_____	5PM_____	"Every day we are given opportunities to organize our time, make choices, and prioritize relationships." p.46
6PM_____	6PM_____	
7PM_____	7PM_____	
8PM_____	8PM_____	

Goals

_____
_____
_____
_____
_____
_____
_____

Action Steps

_____
_____
_____
_____
_____
_____
_____

NOTES

NOTES_____

MONTHLY SELF-REFLECTION:
Measuring the Net Value of Our Choices

What did you discover about yourself from the previous Life Wheel exercise? In what ways did that discovery surprise you? What specific awareness or revelations are most valuable to you?

_____
_____
_____
_____

Which area(s) did you focus on last month? Why?

_____
_____
_____
_____

How were your action steps effective or ineffective? What will you add, alter, or remove about those action steps going forward?

_____
_____
_____
_____

In what ways did having this awareness improve your personal life? Your professional life? The way you lead others?

_____
_____
_____
_____

Knowing we all fall short and have moments we don't achieve our goals and expectations, how will you extend grace to yourself to move forward?

_____
_____
_____
_____

Monthly Life Wheel Exercise

* Feel free to change or add an area. If it's important to you, it's important.

On a scale of one to ten, one being the lowest of the low and ten being best, rate your level of fulfillment in each category and record on the Life Wheel.

Business Calling _____   Financial Health _____

Physical Wellness _____   Relational Health _____

Intimacy _____   Personal Development _____

Play Time/Fun _____   Spiritual Wellness _____

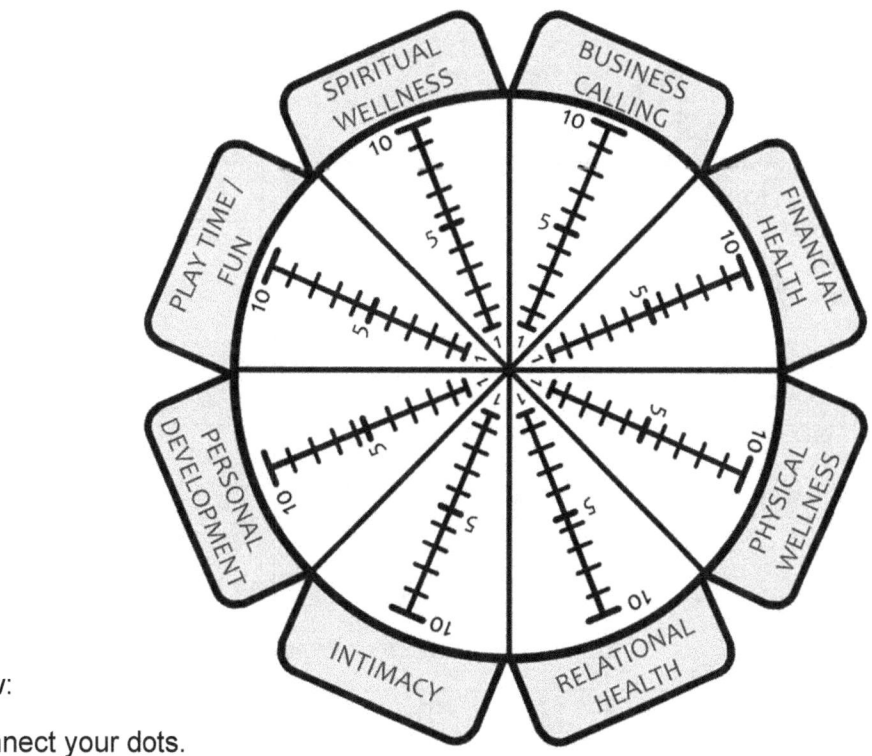

Now:

Connect your dots.

Determine what's on your radar.

What action steps can you take for improvement?

Record your action steps on your month overview. Reassess your steps each week and update accordingly using the central question: In this moment, what choice can I make and what action can I take to create the greatest net value?

Life Wheel Focus Area: *Relational Health: Internal Perspective*
What about this area is important to me?

_____

_____

MONTH: _____   YEAR: _____

Action Steps

_____

_____

_____

_____

_____

_____

_____

_____

_____

_____

_____

OPPORTUNITIES

- ☐ _____
- ☐ _____
- ☐ _____
- ☐ _____
- ☐ _____
- ☐ _____
- ☐ _____
- ☐ _____
- ☐ _____
- ☐ _____

SUNDAY	MONDAY	TUESDAY

NOTES:

Focus Verse: "then make my joy complete by being like-minded, having the same love, being one in spirit and of one mind." Philippians 2:2

How does this verse apply to my internal world?

_____

WEDNESDAY	THURSDAY	FRIDAY	SATURDAY

"I choose how to categorize the file folders of my life stories." p. 133

WEEK OF _____ TO _____

Areas of my Life Wheel on my radar

_____

_____

_____

_____

SUNDAY

9AM_____

10AM_____

11AM_____

12PM_____

1PM_____

2PM_____

3PM_____

4PM_____

5PM_____

6PM_____

MONDAY

5AM_____

6AM_____

7AM_____

8AM_____

9AM_____

10AM_____

11AM_____

12PM_____

1PM_____

2PM_____

3PM_____

4PM_____

5PM_____

6PM_____

7PM_____

8PM_____

TUESDAY

5AM_____

6AM_____

7AM_____

8AM_____

9AM_____

10AM_____

11AM_____

12PM_____

1PM_____

2PM_____

3PM_____

4PM_____

5PM_____

6PM_____

7PM_____

8PM_____

WEDNESDAY

5AM_____

6AM_____

7AM_____

8AM_____

9AM_____

10AM_____

11AM_____

12PM_____

1PM_____

2PM_____

3PM_____

4PM_____

5PM_____

6PM_____

7PM_____

8PM_____

THURSDAY	FRIDAY	SATURDAY
5AM_____	5AM_____	9AM_____
6AM_____	6AM_____	10AM_____
7AM_____	7AM_____	11AM_____
8AM_____	8AM_____	12PM_____
9AM_____	9AM_____	1PM_____
10AM_____	10AM_____	2PM_____
11AM_____	11AM_____	3PM_____
12PM_____	12PM_____	4PM_____
1PM_____	1PM_____	5PM_____
2PM_____	2PM_____	6PM_____
3PM_____	3PM_____	
4PM_____	4PM_____	
5PM_____	5PM_____	"All the pain we feel when we recall our history, how we suffer when organizing our thoughts or experiences, even the discomfort we might feel when we show love – come from the prison cells we created for ourselves." p. 71
6PM_____	6PM_____	
7PM_____	7PM_____	
8PM_____	8PM_____	

Goals

_____
_____
_____
_____
_____
_____
_____

Action Steps

_____
_____
_____
_____
_____
_____

WEEK OF _____ TO _____

Areas of my Life
Wheel on my radar

_____

_____

_____

_____

SUNDAY	MONDAY	TUESDAY	WEDNESDAY
9AM_____	5AM_____	5AM_____	5AM_____
10AM_____	6AM_____	6AM_____	6AM_____
11AM_____	7AM_____	7AM_____	7AM_____
12PM_____	8AM_____	8AM_____	8AM_____
1PM_____	9AM_____	9AM_____	9AM_____
2PM_____	10AM_____	10AM_____	10AM_____
3PM_____	11AM_____	11AM_____	11AM_____
4PM_____	12PM_____	12PM_____	12PM_____
5PM_____	1PM_____	1PM_____	1PM_____
6PM_____	2PM_____	2PM_____	2PM_____
	3PM_____	3PM_____	3PM_____
	4PM_____	4PM_____	4PM_____
	5PM_____	5PM_____	5PM_____
	6PM_____	6PM_____	6PM_____
	7PM_____	7PM_____	7PM_____
	8PM_____	8PM_____	8PM_____

THURSDAY	FRIDAY	SATURDAY
5AM_____	5AM_____	9AM_____
6AM_____	6AM_____	10AM_____
7AM_____	7AM_____	11AM_____
8AM_____	8AM_____	12PM_____
9AM_____	9AM_____	1PM_____
10AM_____	10AM_____	2PM_____
11AM_____	11AM_____	3PM_____
12PM_____	12PM_____	4PM_____
1PM_____	1PM_____	5PM_____
2PM_____	2PM_____	6PM_____
3PM_____	3PM_____	
4PM_____	4PM_____	
5PM_____	5PM_____	
6PM_____	6PM_____	"I choose to tell myself the truth, as it's a critical step to leaving my jail cells." p. 80
7PM_____	7PM_____	
8PM_____	8PM_____	

Goals

_____
_____
_____
_____
_____
_____
_____

Action Steps

_____
_____
_____
_____
_____
_____
_____

WEEK OF _____ TO _____

Areas of my Life Wheel on my radar

_____

_____

_____

_____

SUNDAY
9AM_____
_____
10AM_____
_____
11AM_____
_____
12PM_____
_____
1PM_____
_____
2PM_____
_____
3PM_____
_____
4PM_____
_____
5PM_____
_____
6PM_____
_____

MONDAY	TUESDAY	WEDNESDAY
5AM_____	5AM_____	5AM_____
_____	_____	_____
6AM_____	6AM_____	6AM_____
_____	_____	_____
7AM_____	7AM_____	7AM_____
_____	_____	_____
8AM_____	8AM_____	8AM_____
_____	_____	_____
9AM_____	9AM_____	9AM_____
_____	_____	_____
10AM_____	10AM_____	10AM_____
_____	_____	_____
11AM_____	11AM_____	11AM_____
_____	_____	_____
12PM_____	12PM_____	12PM_____
_____	_____	_____
1PM_____	1PM_____	1PM_____
_____	_____	_____
2PM_____	2PM_____	2PM_____
_____	_____	_____
3PM_____	3PM_____	3PM_____
_____	_____	_____
4PM_____	4PM_____	4PM_____
_____	_____	_____
5PM_____	5PM_____	5PM_____
_____	_____	_____
6PM_____	6PM_____	6PM_____
_____	_____	_____
7PM_____	7PM_____	7PM_____
_____	_____	_____
8PM_____	8PM_____	8PM_____
_____	_____	_____

THURSDAY	FRIDAY	SATURDAY
5AM_____	5AM_____	9AM_____
6AM_____	6AM_____	10AM_____
7AM_____	7AM_____	11AM_____
8AM_____	8AM_____	12PM_____
9AM_____	9AM_____	1PM_____
10AM_____	10AM_____	2PM_____
11AM_____	11AM_____	3PM_____
12PM_____	12PM_____	4PM_____
1PM_____	1PM_____	5PM_____
2PM_____	2PM_____	6PM_____
3PM_____	3PM_____	
4PM_____	4PM_____	
5PM_____	5PM_____	"Am I being who I am called to be in all my interactions, am I showing up and completely present? These are our highest callings of responsibility." p. 93
6PM_____	6PM_____	
7PM_____	7PM_____	
8PM_____	8PM_____	

Goals

_____
_____
_____
_____
_____
_____
_____

Action Steps

_____
_____
_____
_____
_____
_____
_____

WEEK OF _____ TO _____

	MONDAY	TUESDAY	WEDNESDAY

Areas of my Life Wheel on my radar

_____

_____

_____

_____

	MONDAY	TUESDAY	WEDNESDAY
	5AM_____	5AM_____	5AM_____
	6AM_____	6AM_____	6AM_____
	7AM_____	7AM_____	7AM_____
	8AM_____	8AM_____	8AM_____
	9AM_____	9AM_____	9AM_____
	10AM_____	10AM_____	10AM_____
	11AM_____	11AM_____	11AM_____
	12PM_____	12PM_____	12PM_____
	1PM_____	1PM_____	1PM_____
	2PM_____	2PM_____	2PM_____
	3PM_____	3PM_____	3PM_____
	4PM_____	4PM_____	4PM_____
	5PM_____	5PM_____	5PM_____
	6PM_____	6PM_____	6PM_____
	7PM_____	7PM_____	7PM_____
	8PM_____	8PM_____	8PM_____

SUNDAY

9AM_____

10AM_____

11AM_____

12PM_____

1PM_____

2PM_____

3PM_____

4PM_____

5PM_____

6PM_____

THURSDAY	FRIDAY	SATURDAY
5AM_____	5AM_____	9AM_____
6AM_____	6AM_____	10AM_____
7AM_____	7AM_____	11AM_____
8AM_____	8AM_____	12PM_____
9AM_____	9AM_____	1PM_____
10AM_____	10AM_____	2PM_____
11AM_____	11AM_____	3PM_____
12PM_____	12PM_____	4PM_____
1PM_____	1PM_____	5PM_____
2PM_____	2PM_____	6PM_____
3PM_____	3PM_____	
4PM_____	4PM_____	
5PM_____	5PM_____	"Our values are directly linked to, caused by, and affect our thinking patterns. They create the lies we tell ourselves and reinforce through our relationships."
6PM_____	6PM_____	p. 99
7PM_____	7PM_____	
8PM_____	8PM_____	

Goals

_____
_____
_____
_____
_____
_____

Action Steps

_____
_____
_____
_____
_____
_____

WEEK OF _____ TO _____

Areas of my Life
Wheel on my radar

_____

_____

_____

_____

MONDAY	TUESDAY	WEDNESDAY
5AM_____	5AM_____	5AM_____
6AM_____	6AM_____	6AM_____
7AM_____	7AM_____	7AM_____
8AM_____	8AM_____	8AM_____
9AM_____	9AM_____	9AM_____
10AM_____	10AM_____	10AM_____
11AM_____	11AM_____	11AM_____
12PM_____	12PM_____	12PM_____
1PM_____	1PM_____	1PM_____
2PM_____	2PM_____	2PM_____
3PM_____	3PM_____	3PM_____
4PM_____	4PM_____	4PM_____
5PM_____	5PM_____	5PM_____
6PM_____	6PM_____	6PM_____
7PM_____	7PM_____	7PM_____
8PM_____	8PM_____	8PM_____

SUNDAY

9AM_____

10AM_____

11AM_____

12PM_____

1PM_____

2PM_____

3PM_____

4PM_____

5PM_____

6PM_____

THURSDAY	FRIDAY	SATURDAY
5AM_____	5AM_____	9AM_____
6AM_____	6AM_____	10AM_____
7AM_____	7AM_____	11AM_____
8AM_____	8AM_____	12PM_____
9AM_____	9AM_____	1PM_____
10AM_____	10AM_____	2PM_____
11AM_____	11AM_____	3PM_____
12PM_____	12PM_____	4PM_____
1PM_____	1PM_____	5PM_____
2PM_____	2PM_____	6PM_____
3PM_____	3PM_____	
4PM_____	4PM_____	
5PM_____	5PM_____	"When we live a reactionary life, even when we appear to be choosing our experiences, what we're really doing is continually reinforcing our reactions." p. 101
6PM_____	6PM_____	
7PM_____	7PM_____	
8PM_____	8PM_____	

Goals

_____
_____
_____
_____
_____
_____
_____

Action Steps

_____
_____
_____
_____
_____
_____
_____

NOTES_____

REJOICE!

Encourage yourself in your personal and professional life by taking advantage of opportunities to notice and celebrate accomplishments and milestones.

Successes

_____

_____

_____

_____

_____

_____

_____

_____

Completions

_____

_____

_____

_____

_____

_____

_____

_____

Special Events

_____

_____

_____

_____

_____

_____

_____

_____

Memories

_____

_____

_____

_____

_____

_____

_____

_____

MONTHLY SELF-REFLECTION:
Measuring the Net Value of Our Choices

What did you discover about yourself from the previous Life Wheel exercise? In what ways did that discovery surprise you? What specific awareness or revelations are most valuable to you?

_____
_____
_____
_____

Which area(s) did you focus on last month? Why?

_____
_____
_____
_____

How were your action steps effective or ineffective? What will you add, alter, or remove about those action steps going forward?

_____
_____
_____
_____

In what ways did having this awareness improve your personal life? Your professional life? The way you lead others?

_____
_____
_____
_____

Knowing we all fall short and have moments we don't achieve our goals and expectations, how will you extend grace to yourself to move forward?

_____
_____
_____
_____

Monthly Life Wheel Exercise

* Feel free to change or add an area. If it's important to you, it's important.

On a scale of one to ten, one being the lowest of the low and ten being best, rate your level of fulfillment in each category and record on the Life Wheel.

Business Calling _____   Financial Health _____

Physical Wellness _____   Relational Health _____

Intimacy _____   Personal Development _____

Play Time/Fun _____   Spiritual Wellness _____

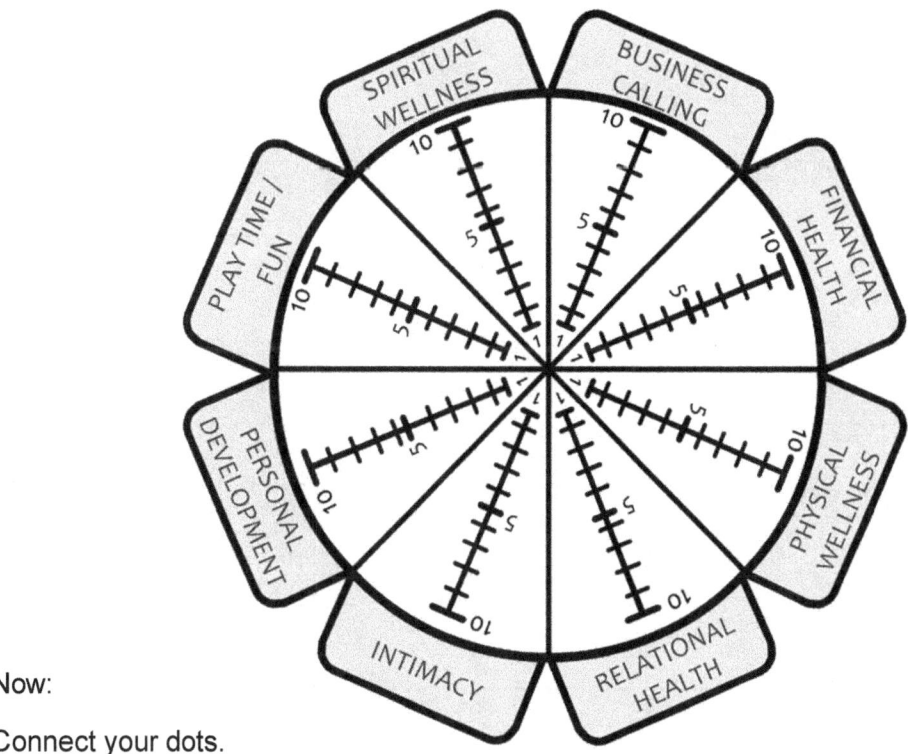

Now:

Connect your dots.

Determine what's on your radar.

What action steps can you take for improvement?

Record your action steps on your month overview. Reassess your steps each week and update accordingly using the central question: In this moment, what choice can I make and what action can I take to create the greatest net value?

Life Wheel Focus Area: *Intimacy: External Perspective*
What about this area is important to me?

_____

_____

MONTH: _____   YEAR: _____

Action Steps

_____
_____
_____
_____
_____
_____
_____
_____
_____
_____
_____

OPPORTUNITIES

- ☐ _____
- ☐ _____
- ☐ _____
- ☐ _____
- ☐ _____
- ☐ _____
- ☐ _____
- ☐ _____
- ☐ _____
- ☐ _____

SUNDAY	MONDAY	TUESDAY

NOTES:

Focus Verse: "After this I looked, and there before me was a great multitude that no one could count, from every nation, tribe, people and language, standing before the throne and before the Lamb." Rev. 7:9a
How does this verse apply to my external world?

_____

WEDNESDAY	THURSDAY	FRIDAY	SATURDAY

"When we reach the deep layer of experience within ourselves, then we can deeply connect with others. This is what our core aches for – authentic connection." p.52

WEEK OF _____ TO _____

Areas of my Life Wheel on my radar

_____

_____

_____

_____

SUNDAY

9AM_____

_____

10AM_____

_____

11AM_____

_____

12PM_____

_____

1PM_____

_____

2PM_____

_____

3PM_____

_____

4PM_____

_____

5PM_____

_____

6PM_____

_____

MONDAY

5AM_____

_____

6AM_____

_____

7AM_____

_____

8AM_____

_____

9AM_____

_____

10AM_____

_____

11AM_____

_____

12PM_____

_____

1PM_____

_____

2PM_____

_____

3PM_____

_____

4PM_____

_____

5PM_____

_____

6PM_____

_____

7PM_____

_____

8PM_____

_____

TUESDAY

5AM_____

_____

6AM_____

_____

7AM_____

_____

8AM_____

_____

9AM_____

_____

10AM_____

_____

11AM_____

_____

12PM_____

_____

1PM_____

_____

2PM_____

_____

3PM_____

_____

4PM_____

_____

5PM_____

_____

6PM_____

_____

7PM_____

_____

8PM_____

_____

WEDNESDAY

5AM_____

_____

6AM_____

_____

7AM_____

_____

8AM_____

_____

9AM_____

_____

10AM_____

_____

11AM_____

_____

12PM_____

_____

1PM_____

_____

2PM_____

_____

3PM_____

_____

4PM_____

_____

5PM_____

_____

6PM_____

_____

7PM_____

_____

8PM_____

_____

THURSDAY	FRIDAY	SATURDAY
5AM_____	5AM_____	9AM_____
6AM_____	6AM_____	10AM_____
7AM_____	7AM_____	11AM_____
8AM_____	8AM_____	12PM_____
9AM_____	9AM_____	1PM_____
10AM_____	10AM_____	2PM_____
11AM_____	11AM_____	3PM_____
12PM_____	12PM_____	4PM_____
1PM_____	1PM_____	5PM_____
2PM_____	2PM_____	6PM_____
3PM_____	3PM_____	
4PM_____	4PM_____	
5PM_____	5PM_____	
6PM_____	6PM_____	"We can reframe our experiences, even the crappiest ones." p. 73
7PM_____	7PM_____	
8PM_____	8PM_____	

Goals

_____
_____
_____
_____
_____
_____
_____

Action Steps

_____
_____
_____
_____
_____
_____
_____
_____

WEEK OF _____ TO _____

Areas of my Life Wheel on my radar

_____

_____

_____

_____

MONDAY	TUESDAY	WEDNESDAY
5AM_____	5AM_____	5AM_____
6AM_____	6AM_____	6AM_____
7AM_____	7AM_____	7AM_____
8AM_____	8AM_____	8AM_____
9AM_____	9AM_____	9AM_____
10AM_____	10AM_____	10AM_____
11AM_____	11AM_____	11AM_____
12PM_____	12PM_____	12PM_____
1PM_____	1PM_____	1PM_____
2PM_____	2PM_____	2PM_____
3PM_____	3PM_____	3PM_____
4PM_____	4PM_____	4PM_____
5PM_____	5PM_____	5PM_____
6PM_____	6PM_____	6PM_____
7PM_____	7PM_____	7PM_____
8PM_____	8PM_____	8PM_____

SUNDAY

9AM_____

10AM_____

11AM_____

12PM_____

1PM_____

2PM_____

3PM_____

4PM_____

5PM_____

6PM_____

THURSDAY	FRIDAY	SATURDAY
5AM_____	5AM_____	9AM_____
6AM_____	6AM_____	10AM_____
7AM_____	7AM_____	11AM_____
8AM_____	8AM_____	12PM_____
9AM_____	9AM_____	1PM_____
10AM_____	10AM_____	2PM_____
11AM_____	11AM_____	3PM_____
12PM_____	12PM_____	4PM_____
1PM_____	1PM_____	5PM_____
2PM_____	2PM_____	6PM_____
3PM_____	3PM_____	
4PM_____	4PM_____	
5PM_____	5PM_____	
6PM_____	6PM_____	"I choose to ask for guidance, help, and support in my journey as needed." p.80
7PM_____	7PM_____	
8PM_____	8PM_____	

Goals

_____

_____

_____

_____

_____

_____

_____

Action Steps

_____

_____

_____

_____

_____

_____

_____

WEEK OF _____ TO _____

Areas of my Life Wheel on my radar

_____

_____

_____

_____

MONDAY

5AM_____

_____

6AM_____

_____

7AM_____

_____

8AM_____

_____

9AM_____

_____

10AM_____

_____

11AM_____

_____

12PM_____

_____

1PM_____

_____

2PM_____

_____

3PM_____

_____

4PM_____

_____

5PM_____

_____

6PM_____

_____

7PM_____

_____

8PM_____

_____

TUESDAY

5AM_____

_____

6AM_____

_____

7AM_____

_____

8AM_____

_____

9AM_____

_____

10AM_____

_____

11AM_____

_____

12PM_____

_____

1PM_____

_____

2PM_____

_____

3PM_____

_____

4PM_____

_____

5PM_____

_____

6PM_____

_____

7PM_____

_____

8PM_____

_____

WEDNESDAY

5AM_____

_____

6AM_____

_____

7AM_____

_____

8AM_____

_____

9AM_____

_____

10AM_____

_____

11AM_____

_____

12PM_____

_____

1PM_____

_____

2PM_____

_____

3PM_____

_____

4PM_____

_____

5PM_____

_____

6PM_____

_____

7PM_____

_____

8PM_____

_____

SUNDAY

9AM_____

_____

10AM_____

_____

11AM_____

_____

12PM_____

_____

1PM_____

_____

2PM_____

_____

3PM_____

_____

4PM_____

_____

5PM_____

_____

6PM_____

_____

THURSDAY	FRIDAY	SATURDAY
5AM_____	5AM_____	9AM_____
6AM_____	6AM_____	10AM_____
7AM_____	7AM_____	11AM_____
8AM_____	8AM_____	12PM_____
9AM_____	9AM_____	1PM_____
10AM_____	10AM_____	2PM_____
11AM_____	11AM_____	3PM_____
12PM_____	12PM_____	4PM_____
1PM_____	1PM_____	5PM_____
2PM_____	2PM_____	6PM_____
3PM_____	3PM_____	
4PM_____	4PM_____	
5PM_____	5PM_____	
6PM_____	6PM_____	"I choose to reframe my crap to fertilizer." p. 80
7PM_____	7PM_____	
8PM_____	8PM_____	

Goals

_____
_____
_____
_____
_____
_____
_____

Action Steps

_____
_____
_____
_____
_____
_____

WEEK OF _____ TO _____

Areas of my Life
Wheel on my radar

_____

_____

_____

_____

SUNDAY	MONDAY	TUESDAY	WEDNESDAY
9AM_____	5AM_____	5AM_____	5AM_____
_____	_____	_____	_____
10AM_____	6AM_____	6AM_____	6AM_____
_____	_____	_____	_____
11AM_____	7AM_____	7AM_____	7AM_____
_____	_____	_____	_____
12PM_____	8AM_____	8AM_____	8AM_____
_____	_____	_____	_____
1PM_____	9AM_____	9AM_____	9AM_____
_____	_____	_____	_____
2PM_____	10AM_____	10AM_____	10AM_____
_____	_____	_____	_____
3PM_____	11AM_____	11AM_____	11AM_____
_____	_____	_____	_____
4PM_____	12PM_____	12PM_____	12PM_____
_____	_____	_____	_____
5PM_____	1PM_____	1PM_____	1PM_____
_____	_____	_____	_____
6PM_____	2PM_____	2PM_____	2PM_____
_____	_____	_____	_____
	3PM_____	3PM_____	3PM_____
	_____	_____	_____
	4PM_____	4PM_____	4PM_____
	_____	_____	_____
	5PM_____	5PM_____	5PM_____
	_____	_____	_____
	6PM_____	6PM_____	6PM_____
	_____	_____	_____
	7PM_____	7PM_____	7PM_____
	_____	_____	_____
	8PM_____	8PM_____	8PM_____
	_____	_____	_____

THURSDAY	FRIDAY	SATURDAY
5AM_____	5AM_____	9AM_____
6AM_____	6AM_____	10AM_____
7AM_____	7AM_____	11AM_____
8AM_____	8AM_____	12PM_____
9AM_____	9AM_____	1PM_____
10AM_____	10AM_____	2PM_____
11AM_____	11AM_____	3PM_____
12PM_____	12PM_____	4PM_____
1PM_____	1PM_____	5PM_____
2PM_____	2PM_____	6PM_____
3PM_____	3PM_____	
4PM_____	4PM_____	
5PM_____	5PM_____	
6PM_____	6PM_____	"I choose to consider ideas I might not otherwise consider." p.133
7PM_____	7PM_____	
8PM_____	8PM_____	

Goals

_____
_____
_____
_____
_____
_____
_____

Action Steps

_____
_____
_____
_____
_____
_____
_____

WEEK OF _____ TO _____

Areas of my Life Wheel on my radar

_____

_____

_____

_____

SUNDAY

9AM_____

_____

10AM_____

_____

11AM_____

_____

12PM_____

_____

1PM_____

_____

2PM_____

_____

3PM_____

_____

4PM_____

_____

5PM_____

_____

6PM_____

_____

MONDAY

5AM_____

_____

6AM_____

_____

7AM_____

_____

8AM_____

_____

9AM_____

_____

10AM_____

_____

11AM_____

_____

12PM_____

_____

1PM_____

_____

2PM_____

_____

3PM_____

_____

4PM_____

_____

5PM_____

_____

6PM_____

_____

7PM_____

_____

8PM_____

_____

TUESDAY

5AM_____

_____

6AM_____

_____

7AM_____

_____

8AM_____

_____

9AM_____

_____

10AM_____

_____

11AM_____

_____

12PM_____

_____

1PM_____

_____

2PM_____

_____

3PM_____

_____

4PM_____

_____

5PM_____

_____

6PM_____

_____

7PM_____

_____

8PM_____

_____

WEDNESDAY

5AM_____

_____

6AM_____

_____

7AM_____

_____

8AM_____

_____

9AM_____

_____

10AM_____

_____

11AM_____

_____

12PM_____

_____

1PM_____

_____

2PM_____

_____

3PM_____

_____

4PM_____

_____

5PM_____

_____

6PM_____

_____

7PM_____

_____

8PM_____

_____

THURSDAY	FRIDAY	SATURDAY
5AM_____	5AM_____	9AM_____
_____	_____	_____
6AM_____	6AM_____	10AM_____
_____	_____	_____
7AM_____	7AM_____	11AM_____
_____	_____	_____
8AM_____	8AM_____	12PM_____
_____	_____	_____
9AM_____	9AM_____	1PM_____
_____	_____	_____
10AM_____	10AM_____	2PM_____
_____	_____	_____
11AM_____	11AM_____	3PM_____
_____	_____	_____
12PM_____	12PM_____	4PM_____
_____	_____	_____
1PM_____	1PM_____	5PM_____
_____	_____	_____
2PM_____	2PM_____	6PM_____
_____	_____	_____
3PM_____	3PM_____	
_____	_____	
4PM_____	4PM_____	
_____	_____	
5PM_____	5PM_____	"Being whom you choose and want to be requires a daily commitment to inner personal integrity with yourself, and authenticity with those in your world." p. 91
_____	_____	
6PM_____	6PM_____	
_____	_____	
7PM_____	7PM_____	
_____	_____	
8PM_____	8PM_____	
_____	_____	

Goals

_____

_____

_____

_____

_____

_____

_____

_____

Action Steps

_____

_____

_____

_____

_____

_____

_____

NOTES_____

NOTES

MONTHLY SELF-REFLECTION:
Measuring the Net Value of Our Choices

What did you discover about yourself from the previous Life Wheel exercise? In what ways did that discovery surprise you? What specific awareness or revelations are most valuable to you?

_____

_____

_____

_____

Which area(s) did you focus on last month? Why?

_____

_____

_____

_____

How were your action steps effective or ineffective? What will you add, alter, or remove about those action steps going forward?

_____

_____

_____

_____

In what ways did having this awareness improve your personal life? Your professional life? The way you lead others?

_____

_____

_____

_____

Knowing we all fall short and have moments we don't achieve our goals and expectations, how will you extend grace to yourself to move forward?

_____

_____

_____

_____

Monthly Life Wheel Exercise

* Feel free to change or add an area. If it's important to you, it's important.

On a scale of one to ten, one being the lowest of the low and ten being best, rate your level of fulfillment in each category and record on the Life Wheel.

Business Calling _____   Financial Health _____

Physical Wellness _____   Relational Health _____

Intimacy _____   Personal Development _____

Play Time/Fun _____   Spiritual Wellness _____

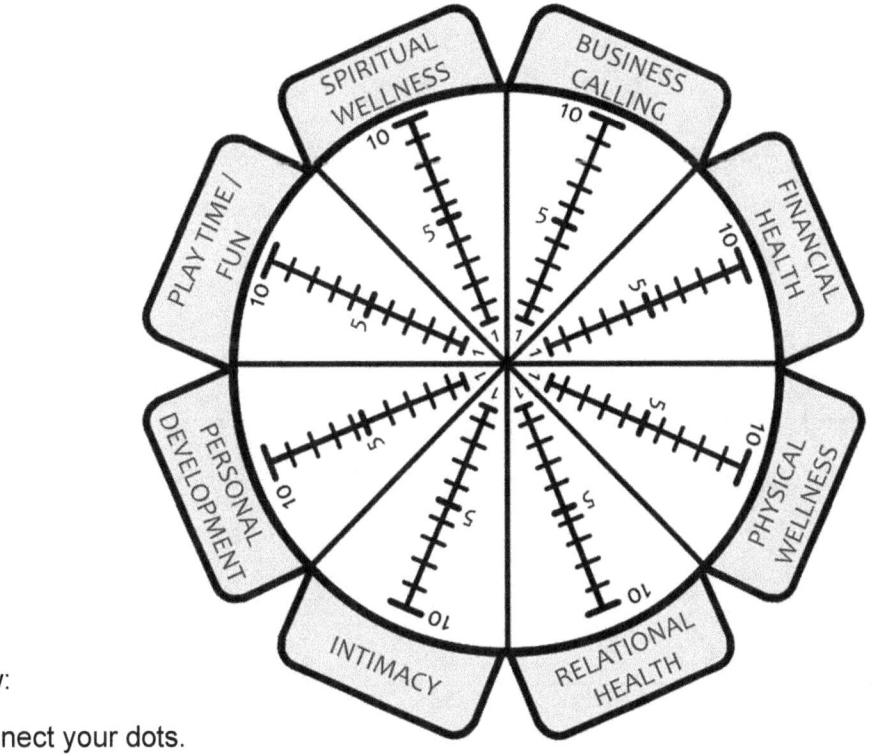

Now:

Connect your dots.

Determine what's on your radar.

What action steps can you take for improvement?

Record your action steps on your month overview. Reassess your steps each week and update accordingly using the central question: In this moment, what choice can I make and what action can I take to create the greatest net value?

Life Wheel Focus Area: *Intimacy: Internal Perspective*

What about this area is important to me?

_____

_____

MONTH: _____   YEAR: _____

Action Steps

_____
_____
_____
_____
_____
_____
_____
_____
_____
_____
_____
_____
_____

OPPORTUNITIES

- ☐ _____
- ☐ _____
- ☐ _____
- ☐ _____
- ☐ _____
- ☐ _____
- ☐ _____
- ☐ _____
- ☐ _____
- ☐ _____

SUNDAY	MONDAY	TUESDAY

NOTES:

Focus Verse: "Neither height nor depth, nor anything else in all creation, will be able to separate us from the love of God that is in Christ Jesus our Lord."
Romans 8:39
How does this verse apply to my internal world?

_____

WEDNESDAY	THURSDAY	FRIDAY	SATURDAY

"I choose to recognize some of my jail cells are of my own making." p.80

WEEK OF _____ TO _____

Areas of my Life Wheel on my radar

_____
_____
_____
_____

SUNDAY
9AM_____
_____
10AM_____
_____
11AM_____
_____
12PM_____
_____
1PM_____
_____
2PM_____
_____
3PM_____
_____
4PM_____
_____
5PM_____
_____
6PM_____
_____

MONDAY	TUESDAY	WEDNESDAY
5AM_____	5AM_____	5AM_____
_____	_____	_____
6AM_____	6AM_____	6AM_____
_____	_____	_____
7AM_____	7AM_____	7AM_____
_____	_____	_____
8AM_____	8AM_____	8AM_____
_____	_____	_____
9AM_____	9AM_____	9AM_____
_____	_____	_____
10AM_____	10AM_____	10AM_____
_____	_____	_____
11AM_____	11AM_____	11AM_____
_____	_____	_____
12PM_____	12PM_____	12PM_____
_____	_____	_____
1PM_____	1PM_____	1PM_____
_____	_____	_____
2PM_____	2PM_____	2PM_____
_____	_____	_____
3PM_____	3PM_____	3PM_____
_____	_____	_____
4PM_____	4PM_____	4PM_____
_____	_____	_____
5PM_____	5PM_____	5PM_____
_____	_____	_____
6PM_____	6PM_____	6PM_____
_____	_____	_____
7PM_____	7PM_____	7PM_____
_____	_____	_____
8PM_____	8PM_____	8PM_____
_____	_____	_____

THURSDAY	FRIDAY	SATURDAY
5AM_____	5AM_____	9AM_____
6AM_____	6AM_____	10AM_____
7AM_____	7AM_____	11AM_____
8AM_____	8AM_____	12PM_____
9AM_____	9AM_____	1PM_____
10AM_____	10AM_____	2PM_____
11AM_____	11AM_____	3PM_____
12PM_____	12PM_____	4PM_____
1PM_____	1PM_____	5PM_____
2PM_____	2PM_____	6PM_____
3PM_____	3PM_____	
4PM_____	4PM_____	
5PM_____	5PM_____	"I choose to acknowledge I hold the key to each layer and each lock."
6PM_____	6PM_____	p. 80
7PM_____	7PM_____	
8PM_____	8PM_____	

Goals

_____
_____
_____
_____
_____
_____
_____

Action Steps

_____
_____
_____
_____
_____
_____
_____

WEEK OF _____ TO _____

Areas of my Life Wheel on my radar	MONDAY	TUESDAY	WEDNESDAY
_____	5AM_____	5AM_____	5AM_____
_____	6AM_____	6AM_____	6AM_____
_____	7AM_____	7AM_____	7AM_____
_____	8AM_____	8AM_____	8AM_____
	9AM_____	9AM_____	9AM_____
	10AM_____	10AM_____	10AM_____

SUNDAY			
9AM_____	11AM_____	11AM_____	11AM_____
10AM_____	12PM_____	12PM_____	12PM_____
11AM_____	1PM_____	1PM_____	1PM_____
12PM_____	2PM_____	2PM_____	2PM_____
1PM_____	3PM_____	3PM_____	3PM_____
2PM_____	4PM_____	4PM_____	4PM_____
3PM_____	5PM_____	5PM_____	5PM_____
4PM_____	6PM_____	6PM_____	6PM_____
5PM_____	7PM_____	7PM_____	7PM_____
6PM_____	8PM_____	8PM_____	8PM_____

THURSDAY	FRIDAY	SATURDAY
5AM_____	5AM_____	9AM_____
6AM_____	6AM_____	10AM_____
7AM_____	7AM_____	11AM_____
8AM_____	8AM_____	12PM_____
9AM_____	9AM_____	1PM_____
10AM_____	10AM_____	2PM_____
11AM_____	11AM_____	3PM_____
12PM_____	12PM_____	4PM_____
1PM_____	1PM_____	5PM_____
2PM_____	2PM_____	6PM_____
3PM_____	3PM_____	
4PM_____	4PM_____	
5PM_____	5PM_____	
6PM_____	6PM_____	"I choose when I am ready to open each door." p.80
7PM_____	7PM_____	
8PM_____	8PM_____	

Goals

_____
_____
_____
_____
_____
_____
_____

Action Steps

_____
_____
_____
_____
_____
_____
_____

WEEK OF _____ TO _____

Areas of my Life Wheel on my radar

_____

_____

_____

_____

MONDAY	TUESDAY	WEDNESDAY
5AM_____	5AM_____	5AM_____
_____	_____	_____
6AM_____	6AM_____	6AM_____
_____	_____	_____
7AM_____	7AM_____	7AM_____
_____	_____	_____
8AM_____	8AM_____	8AM_____
_____	_____	_____
9AM_____	9AM_____	9AM_____
_____	_____	_____
10AM_____	10AM_____	10AM_____
_____	_____	_____
11AM_____	11AM_____	11AM_____
_____	_____	_____
12PM_____	12PM_____	12PM_____
_____	_____	_____
1PM_____	1PM_____	1PM_____
_____	_____	_____
2PM_____	2PM_____	2PM_____
_____	_____	_____
3PM_____	3PM_____	3PM_____
_____	_____	_____
4PM_____	4PM_____	4PM_____
_____	_____	_____
5PM_____	5PM_____	5PM_____
_____	_____	_____
6PM_____	6PM_____	6PM_____
_____	_____	_____
7PM_____	7PM_____	7PM_____
_____	_____	_____
8PM_____	8PM_____	8PM_____
_____	_____	_____

SUNDAY

9AM_____

_____

10AM_____

_____

11AM_____

_____

12PM_____

_____

1PM_____

_____

2PM_____

_____

3PM_____

_____

4PM_____

_____

5PM_____

_____

6PM_____

_____

THURSDAY	FRIDAY	SATURDAY
5AM_____	5AM_____	9AM_____
6AM_____	6AM_____	10AM_____
7AM_____	7AM_____	11AM_____
8AM_____	8AM_____	12PM_____
9AM_____	9AM_____	1PM_____
10AM_____	10AM_____	2PM_____
11AM_____	11AM_____	3PM_____
12PM_____	12PM_____	4PM_____
1PM_____	1PM_____	5PM_____
2PM_____	2PM_____	6PM_____
3PM_____	3PM_____	
4PM_____	4PM_____	
5PM_____	5PM_____	"Many people find manifesting personal integrity within themselves is immensely difficult." p. 82
6PM_____	6PM_____	
7PM_____	7PM_____	
8PM_____	8PM_____	

Goals

_____
_____
_____
_____
_____
_____
_____

Action Steps

_____
_____
_____
_____
_____
_____
_____

WEEK OF _____ TO _____

Areas of my Life Wheel on my radar

_____

_____

_____

_____

MONDAY	TUESDAY	WEDNESDAY
5AM_____	5AM_____	5AM_____
_____	_____	_____
6AM_____	6AM_____	6AM_____
_____	_____	_____
7AM_____	7AM_____	7AM_____
_____	_____	_____
8AM_____	8AM_____	8AM_____
_____	_____	_____
9AM_____	9AM_____	9AM_____
_____	_____	_____
10AM_____	10AM_____	10AM_____
_____	_____	_____
11AM_____	11AM_____	11AM_____
_____	_____	_____
12PM_____	12PM_____	12PM_____
_____	_____	_____
1PM_____	1PM_____	1PM_____
_____	_____	_____
2PM_____	2PM_____	2PM_____
_____	_____	_____
3PM_____	3PM_____	3PM_____
_____	_____	_____
4PM_____	4PM_____	4PM_____
_____	_____	_____
5PM_____	5PM_____	5PM_____
_____	_____	_____
6PM_____	6PM_____	6PM_____
_____	_____	_____
7PM_____	7PM_____	7PM_____
_____	_____	_____
8PM_____	8PM_____	8PM_____
_____	_____	_____

SUNDAY

9AM_____

_____

10AM_____

_____

11AM_____

_____

12PM_____

_____

1PM_____

_____

2PM_____

_____

3PM_____

_____

4PM_____

_____

5PM_____

_____

6PM_____

_____

THURSDAY	FRIDAY	SATURDAY
5AM_____	5AM_____	9AM_____
6AM_____	6AM_____	10AM_____
7AM_____	7AM_____	11AM_____
8AM_____	8AM_____	12PM_____
9AM_____	9AM_____	1PM_____
10AM_____	10AM_____	2PM_____
11AM_____	11AM_____	3PM_____
12PM_____	12PM_____	4PM_____
1PM_____	1PM_____	5PM_____
2PM_____	2PM_____	6PM_____
3PM_____	3PM_____	
4PM_____	4PM_____	
5PM_____	5PM_____	
6PM_____	6PM_____	"I choose to seek on-going revelation of my layers to unlock more jail cells." p. 160
7PM_____	7PM_____	
8PM_____	8PM_____	

Goals

_____
_____
_____
_____
_____
_____
_____

Action Steps

_____
_____
_____
_____
_____
_____
_____

WEEK OF _____ TO _____

Areas of my Life Wheel on my radar	MONDAY	TUESDAY	WEDNESDAY
_____	5AM_____	5AM_____	5AM_____
_____	6AM_____	6AM_____	6AM_____
_____	7AM_____	7AM_____	7AM_____
_____	8AM_____	8AM_____	8AM_____
	9AM_____	9AM_____	9AM_____
SUNDAY	10AM_____	10AM_____	10AM_____
9AM_____	11AM_____	11AM_____	11AM_____
10AM_____	12PM_____	12PM_____	12PM_____
11AM_____	1PM_____	1PM_____	1PM_____
12PM_____	2PM_____	2PM_____	2PM_____
1PM_____	3PM_____	3PM_____	3PM_____
2PM_____	4PM_____	4PM_____	4PM_____
3PM_____	5PM_____	5PM_____	5PM_____
4PM_____	6PM_____	6PM_____	6PM_____
5PM_____	7PM_____	7PM_____	7PM_____
6PM_____	8PM_____	8PM_____	8PM_____

THURSDAY	FRIDAY	SATURDAY
5AM_____	5AM_____	9AM_____
6AM_____	6AM_____	10AM_____
7AM_____	7AM_____	11AM_____
8AM_____	8AM_____	12PM_____
9AM_____	9AM_____	1PM_____
10AM_____	10AM_____	2PM_____
11AM_____	11AM_____	3PM_____
12PM_____	12PM_____	4PM_____
1PM_____	1PM_____	5PM_____
2PM_____	2PM_____	6PM_____
3PM_____	3PM_____	
4PM_____	4PM_____	
5PM_____	5PM_____	"I can choose to add habits to increase my satisfaction and results. Connecting my Life Wheel results with actions helps me avoid indecision and move forward." p. 143
6PM_____	6PM_____	
7PM_____	7PM_____	
8PM_____	8PM_____	

Goals

_____
_____
_____
_____
_____
_____
_____

Action Steps

_____
_____
_____
_____
_____
_____
_____

NOTES_____
_____
_____
_____
_____
_____
_____
_____
_____
_____
_____
_____
_____
_____
_____
_____
_____
_____
_____
_____
_____
_____
_____
_____
_____
_____
_____
_____
_____
_____
_____
_____
_____
_____
_____
_____
_____
_____
_____
_____
_____

NOTES

MONTHLY SELF-REFLECTION:
Measuring the Net Value of Our Choices

What did you discover about yourself from the previous Life Wheel exercise? In what ways did that discovery surprise you? What specific awareness or revelations are most valuable to you?

_____
_____
_____
_____

Which area(s) did you focus on last month? Why?

_____
_____
_____
_____

How were your action steps effective or ineffective? What will you add, alter, or remove about those action steps going forward?

_____
_____
_____
_____

In what ways did having this awareness improve your personal life? Your professional life? The way you lead others?

_____
_____
_____
_____

Knowing we all fall short and have moments we don't achieve our goals and expectations, how will you extend grace to yourself to move forward?

_____
_____
_____
_____

Monthly Life Wheel Exercise

* Feel free to change or add an area. If it's important to you, it's important.

On a scale of one to ten, one being the lowest of the low and ten being best, rate your level of fulfillment in each category and record on the Life Wheel.

Business Calling _____   Financial Health _____

Physical Wellness _____   Relational Health _____

Intimacy _____   Personal Development _____

Play Time/Fun _____   Spiritual Wellness _____

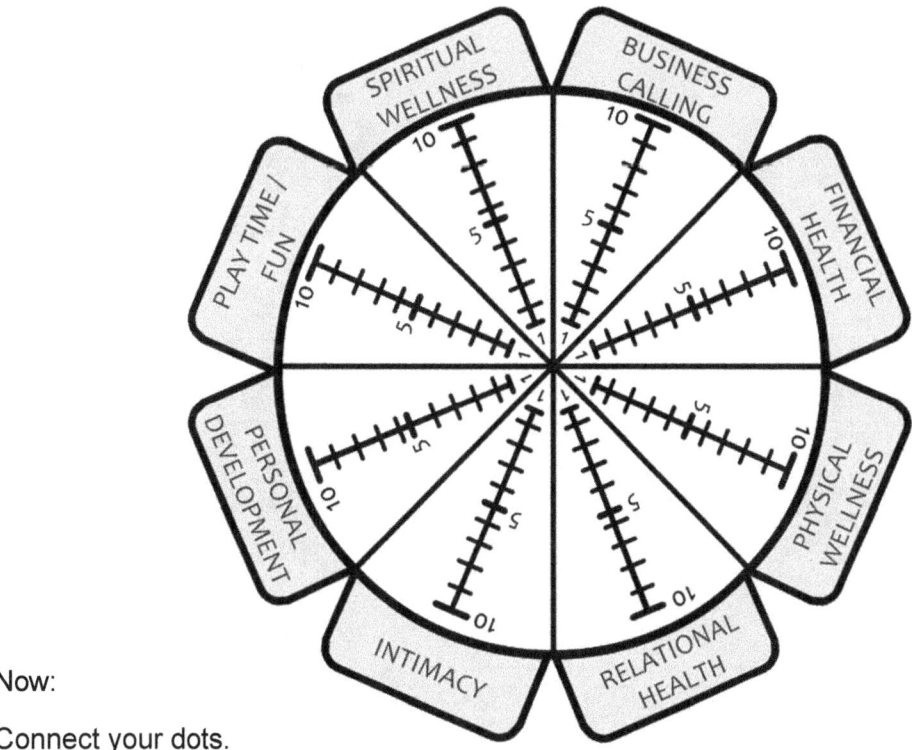

Now:

Connect your dots.

Determine what's on your radar.

What action steps can you take for improvement?

Record your action steps on your month overview. Reassess your steps each week and update accordingly using the central question: In this moment, what choice can I make and what action can I take to create the greatest net value?

Life Wheel Focus Area: *Personal Development: External Perspective*

What about this area is important to me?

_____

_____

MONTH: _____   YEAR: _____

Action Steps

_____
_____
_____
_____
_____
_____
_____
_____
_____
_____
_____

OPPORTUNITIES

☐ _____
☐ _____
☐ _____
☐ _____
☐ _____
☐ _____
☐ _____
☐ _____
☐ _____
☐ _____

SUNDAY	MONDAY	TUESDAY

NOTES:

Focus Verse: "Very truly I tell you, whoever believes in me will do the works I have been doing, and they will do even greater things than these, because I am going to the Father." John 14:12

How does this verse apply to my external world?

_____

WEDNESDAY	THURSDAY	FRIDAY	SATURDAY

"Our beliefs, thoughts, words, actions, habits, and values all have power we can harness." p. 69

WEEK OF _____ TO _____

	MONDAY	TUESDAY	WEDNESDAY

Areas of my Life Wheel on my radar

_____
_____
_____
_____

SUNDAY

9AM_____
_____
10AM_____
_____
11AM_____
_____
12PM_____
_____
1PM_____
_____
2PM_____
_____
3PM_____
_____
4PM_____
_____
5PM_____
_____
6PM_____
_____

MONDAY

5AM_____
_____
6AM_____
_____
7AM_____
_____
8AM_____
_____
9AM_____
_____
10AM_____
_____
11AM_____
_____
12PM_____
_____
1PM_____
_____
2PM_____
_____
3PM_____
_____
4PM_____
_____
5PM_____
_____
6PM_____
_____
7PM_____
_____
8PM_____
_____

TUESDAY

5AM_____
_____
6AM_____
_____
7AM_____
_____
8AM_____
_____
9AM_____
_____
10AM_____
_____
11AM_____
_____
12PM_____
_____
1PM_____
_____
2PM_____
_____
3PM_____
_____
4PM_____
_____
5PM_____
_____
6PM_____
_____
7PM_____
_____
8PM_____
_____

WEDNESDAY

5AM_____
_____
6AM_____
_____
7AM_____
_____
8AM_____
_____
9AM_____
_____
10AM_____
_____
11AM_____
_____
12PM_____
_____
1PM_____
_____
2PM_____
_____
3PM_____
_____
4PM_____
_____
5PM_____
_____
6PM_____
_____
7PM_____
_____
8PM_____
_____

THURSDAY	FRIDAY	SATURDAY
5AM_____	5AM_____	9AM_____
6AM_____	6AM_____	10AM_____
7AM_____	7AM_____	11AM_____
8AM_____	8AM_____	12PM_____
9AM_____	9AM_____	1PM_____
10AM_____	10AM_____	2PM_____
11AM_____	11AM_____	3PM_____
12PM_____	12PM_____	4PM_____
1PM_____	1PM_____	5PM_____
2PM_____	2PM_____	6PM_____
3PM_____	3PM_____	
4PM_____	4PM_____	
5PM_____	5PM_____	
6PM_____	6PM_____	"Our heart, mind, and soul are our layers." p.8
7PM_____	7PM_____	
8PM_____	8PM_____	

Goals

_____
_____
_____
_____
_____
_____
_____

Action Steps

_____
_____
_____
_____
_____
_____
_____

WEEK OF _____ TO _____

SUNDAY	MONDAY	TUESDAY	WEDNESDAY
9AM_____	5AM_____	5AM_____	5AM_____
_____	_____	_____	_____
10AM_____	6AM_____	6AM_____	6AM_____
_____	_____	_____	_____
11AM_____	7AM_____	7AM_____	7AM_____
_____	_____	_____	_____
12PM_____	8AM_____	8AM_____	8AM_____
_____	_____	_____	_____
1PM_____	9AM_____	9AM_____	9AM_____
_____	_____	_____	_____
2PM_____	10AM_____	10AM_____	10AM_____
_____	_____	_____	_____
3PM_____	11AM_____	11AM_____	11AM_____
_____	_____	_____	_____
4PM_____	12PM_____	12PM_____	12PM_____
_____	_____	_____	_____
5PM_____	1PM_____	1PM_____	1PM_____
_____	_____	_____	_____
6PM_____	2PM_____	2PM_____	2PM_____
_____	_____	_____	_____
	3PM_____	3PM_____	3PM_____
	_____	_____	_____
	4PM_____	4PM_____	4PM_____
	_____	_____	_____
	5PM_____	5PM_____	5PM_____
	_____	_____	_____
	6PM_____	6PM_____	6PM_____
	_____	_____	_____
	7PM_____	7PM_____	7PM_____
	_____	_____	_____
	8PM_____	8PM_____	8PM_____
	_____	_____	_____

THURSDAY	FRIDAY	SATURDAY
5AM_____	5AM_____	9AM_____
_____	_____	_____
6AM_____	6AM_____	10AM_____
_____	_____	_____
7AM_____	7AM_____	11AM_____
_____	_____	_____
8AM_____	8AM_____	12PM_____
_____	_____	_____
9AM_____	9AM_____	1PM_____
_____	_____	_____
10AM_____	10AM_____	2PM_____
_____	_____	_____
11AM_____	11AM_____	3PM_____
_____	_____	_____
12PM_____	12PM_____	4PM_____
_____	_____	_____
1PM_____	1PM_____	5PM_____
_____	_____	_____
2PM_____	2PM_____	6PM_____
_____	_____	_____
3PM_____	3PM_____	
_____	_____	
4PM_____	4PM_____	
_____	_____	
5PM_____	5PM_____	
_____	_____	"We are all like onions. The layers are many, and slaying is a lifelong process." p. 146
6PM_____	6PM_____	
_____	_____	
7PM_____	7PM_____	
_____	_____	
8PM_____	8PM_____	
_____	_____	

Goals

_____
_____
_____
_____
_____
_____
_____

Action Steps

_____
_____
_____
_____
_____
_____
_____

WEEK OF _____ TO _____

Areas of my Life Wheel on my radar

_____

_____

_____

_____

MONDAY	TUESDAY	WEDNESDAY
5AM_____	5AM_____	5AM_____
6AM_____	6AM_____	6AM_____
7AM_____	7AM_____	7AM_____
8AM_____	8AM_____	8AM_____
9AM_____	9AM_____	9AM_____
10AM_____	10AM_____	10AM_____
11AM_____	11AM_____	11AM_____
12PM_____	12PM_____	12PM_____
1PM_____	1PM_____	1PM_____
2PM_____	2PM_____	2PM_____
3PM_____	3PM_____	3PM_____
4PM_____	4PM_____	4PM_____
5PM_____	5PM_____	5PM_____
6PM_____	6PM_____	6PM_____
7PM_____	7PM_____	7PM_____
8PM_____	8PM_____	8PM_____

SUNDAY

9AM_____

10AM_____

11AM_____

12PM_____

1PM_____

2PM_____

3PM_____

4PM_____

5PM_____

6PM_____

THURSDAY	FRIDAY	SATURDAY
5AM_____	5AM_____	9AM_____
6AM_____	6AM_____	10AM_____
7AM_____	7AM_____	11AM_____
8AM_____	8AM_____	12PM_____
9AM_____	9AM_____	1PM_____
10AM_____	10AM_____	2PM_____
11AM_____	11AM_____	3PM_____
12PM_____	12PM_____	4PM_____
1PM_____	1PM_____	5PM_____
2PM_____	2PM_____	6PM_____
3PM_____	3PM_____	
4PM_____	4PM_____	
5PM_____	5PM_____	"We get to choose our path, even if we choose not to choose. And every choice has its consequences and rewards." p. 128
6PM_____	6PM_____	
7PM_____	7PM_____	
8PM_____	8PM_____	

Goals

_____
_____
_____
_____
_____
_____
_____

Action Steps

_____
_____
_____
_____
_____
_____
_____

WEEK OF _____ TO _____

Areas of my Life
Wheel on my radar

_____

_____

_____

_____

SUNDAY

9AM_____

_____

10AM_____

_____

11AM_____

_____

12PM_____

_____

1PM_____

_____

2PM_____

_____

3PM_____

_____

4PM_____

_____

5PM_____

_____

6PM_____

_____

MONDAY	TUESDAY	WEDNESDAY
5AM_____	5AM_____	5AM_____
_____	_____	_____
6AM_____	6AM_____	6AM_____
_____	_____	_____
7AM_____	7AM_____	7AM_____
_____	_____	_____
8AM_____	8AM_____	8AM_____
_____	_____	_____
9AM_____	9AM_____	9AM_____
_____	_____	_____
10AM_____	10AM_____	10AM_____
_____	_____	_____
11AM_____	11AM_____	11AM_____
_____	_____	_____
12PM_____	12PM_____	12PM_____
_____	_____	_____
1PM_____	1PM_____	1PM_____
_____	_____	_____
2PM_____	2PM_____	2PM_____
_____	_____	_____
3PM_____	3PM_____	3PM_____
_____	_____	_____
4PM_____	4PM_____	4PM_____
_____	_____	_____
5PM_____	5PM_____	5PM_____
_____	_____	_____
6PM_____	6PM_____	6PM_____
_____	_____	_____
7PM_____	7PM_____	7PM_____
_____	_____	_____
8PM_____	8PM_____	8PM_____
_____	_____	_____

THURSDAY	FRIDAY	SATURDAY
5AM_____	5AM_____	9AM_____
6AM_____	6AM_____	10AM_____
7AM_____	7AM_____	11AM_____
8AM_____	8AM_____	12PM_____
9AM_____	9AM_____	1PM_____
10AM_____	10AM_____	2PM_____
11AM_____	11AM_____	3PM_____
12PM_____	12PM_____	4PM_____
1PM_____	1PM_____	5PM_____
2PM_____	2PM_____	6PM_____
3PM_____	3PM_____	
4PM_____	4PM_____	
5PM_____	5PM_____	"When we give someone permission to walk inside our layers they leave a mark – an indent, or possibly, a gift." p. 129
6PM_____	6PM_____	
7PM_____	7PM_____	
8PM_____	8PM_____	

Goals

_____
_____
_____
_____
_____
_____
_____

Action Steps

_____
_____
_____
_____
_____
_____
_____

WEEK OF _____ TO _____

Areas of my Life
Wheel on my radar

_____

_____

_____

_____

MONDAY	TUESDAY	WEDNESDAY
5AM_____	5AM_____	5AM_____
6AM_____	6AM_____	6AM_____
7AM_____	7AM_____	7AM_____
8AM_____	8AM_____	8AM_____
9AM_____	9AM_____	9AM_____
10AM_____	10AM_____	10AM_____
11AM_____	11AM_____	11AM_____
12PM_____	12PM_____	12PM_____
1PM_____	1PM_____	1PM_____
2PM_____	2PM_____	2PM_____
3PM_____	3PM_____	3PM_____
4PM_____	4PM_____	4PM_____
5PM_____	5PM_____	5PM_____
6PM_____	6PM_____	6PM_____
7PM_____	7PM_____	7PM_____
8PM_____	8PM_____	8PM_____

SUNDAY

9AM_____

10AM_____

11AM_____

12PM_____

1PM_____

2PM_____

3PM_____

4PM_____

5PM_____

6PM_____

THURSDAY	FRIDAY	SATURDAY
5AM_____	5AM_____	9AM_____
6AM_____	6AM_____	10AM_____
7AM_____	7AM_____	11AM_____
8AM_____	8AM_____	12PM_____
9AM_____	9AM_____	1PM_____
10AM_____	10AM_____	2PM_____
11AM_____	11AM_____	3PM_____
12PM_____	12PM_____	4PM_____
1PM_____	1PM_____	5PM_____
2PM_____	2PM_____	6PM_____
3PM_____	3PM_____	
4PM_____	4PM_____	
5PM_____	5PM_____	"I choose to pursue living in agape love with myself." p. 60
6PM_____	6PM_____	
7PM_____	7PM_____	
8PM_____	8PM_____	

Goals

_____
_____
_____
_____
_____
_____
_____

Action Steps

_____
_____
_____
_____
_____
_____
_____

NOTES_____

NOTES

MONTHLY SELF-REFLECTION:
Measuring the Net Value of Our Choices

What did you discover about yourself from the previous Life Wheel exercise? In what ways did that discovery surprise you? What specific awareness or revelations are most valuable to you?

_____

_____

_____

_____

Which area(s) did you focus on last month? Why?

_____

_____

_____

_____

How were your action steps effective or ineffective? What will you add, alter, or remove about those action steps going forward?

_____

_____

_____

_____

In what ways did having this awareness improve your personal life? Your professional life? The way you lead others?

_____

_____

_____

_____

Knowing we all fall short and have moments we don't achieve our goals and expectations, how will you extend grace to yourself to move forward?

_____

_____

_____

_____

Monthly Life Wheel Exercise

* Feel free to change or add an area. If it's important to you, it's important.

On a scale of one to ten, one being the lowest of the low and ten being best, rate your level of fulfillment in each category and record on the Life Wheel.

Business Calling _____   Financial Health _____

Physical Wellness _____   Relational Health _____

Intimacy _____   Personal Development _____

Play Time/Fun _____   Spiritual Wellness _____

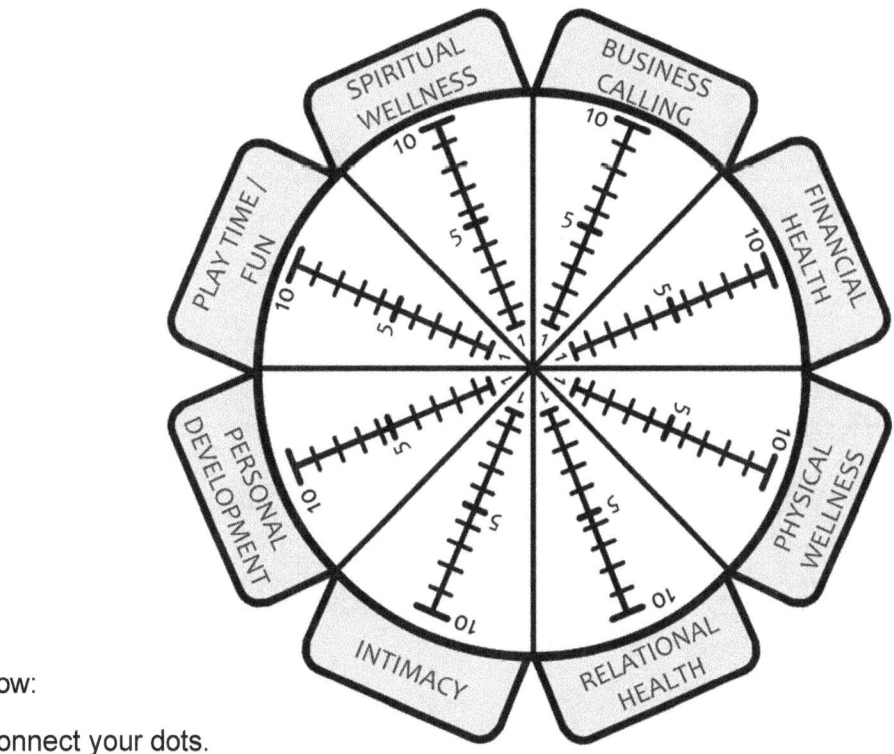

Now:

Connect your dots.

Determine what's on your radar.

What action steps can you take for improvement?

Record your action steps on your month overview. Reassess your steps each week and update accordingly using the central question: In this moment, what choice can I make and what action can I take to create the greatest net value?

Life Wheel Focus Area: *Personal Development: Internal Perspective*
What about this area is important to me?

_____

_____

MONTH: _____   YEAR: _____

Action Steps

_____

_____

_____

_____

_____

_____

_____

_____

_____

_____

_____

_____

OPPORTUNITIES

- ☐ _____
- ☐ _____
- ☐ _____
- ☐ _____
- ☐ _____
- ☐ _____
- ☐ _____
- ☐ _____
- ☐ _____
- ☐ _____

SUNDAY	MONDAY	TUESDAY

NOTES:

Focus Verse: "And again, 'I will put my trust in him.' And again he says, 'Here am I, and the children God has given me.'" Hebrews 2:13

How does this verse apply to my external world?

_____

WEDNESDAY	THURSDAY	FRIDAY	SATURDAY

"We can ultimately choose to respond negatively or positively, no matter the event." p. 51

WEEK OF _____ TO _____

Areas of my Life Wheel on my radar

_____

_____

_____

_____

SUNDAY

9AM_____

_____

10AM_____

_____

11AM_____

_____

12PM_____

_____

1PM_____

_____

2PM_____

_____

3PM_____

_____

4PM_____

_____

5PM_____

_____

6PM_____

_____

MONDAY

5AM_____

_____

6AM_____

_____

7AM_____

_____

8AM_____

_____

9AM_____

_____

10AM_____

_____

11AM_____

_____

12PM_____

_____

1PM_____

_____

2PM_____

_____

3PM_____

_____

4PM_____

_____

5PM_____

_____

6PM_____

_____

7PM_____

_____

8PM_____

_____

TUESDAY

5AM_____

_____

6AM_____

_____

7AM_____

_____

8AM_____

_____

9AM_____

_____

10AM_____

_____

11AM_____

_____

12PM_____

_____

1PM_____

_____

2PM_____

_____

3PM_____

_____

4PM_____

_____

5PM_____

_____

6PM_____

_____

7PM_____

_____

8PM_____

_____

WEDNESDAY

5AM_____

_____

6AM_____

_____

7AM_____

_____

8AM_____

_____

9AM_____

_____

10AM_____

_____

11AM_____

_____

12PM_____

_____

1PM_____

_____

2PM_____

_____

3PM_____

_____

4PM_____

_____

5PM_____

_____

6PM_____

_____

7PM_____

_____

8PM_____

_____

THURSDAY	FRIDAY	SATURDAY
5AM_____	5AM_____	9AM_____
6AM_____	6AM_____	10AM_____
7AM_____	7AM_____	11AM_____
8AM_____	8AM_____	12PM_____
9AM_____	9AM_____	1PM_____
10AM_____	10AM_____	2PM_____
11AM_____	11AM_____	3PM_____
12PM_____	12PM_____	4PM_____
1PM_____	1PM_____	5PM_____
2PM_____	2PM_____	6PM_____
3PM_____	3PM_____	
4PM_____	4PM_____	
5PM_____	5PM_____	"I choose to be responsible for my choices." p. 105
6PM_____	6PM_____	
7PM_____	7PM_____	
8PM_____	8PM_____	

Goals

_____
_____
_____
_____
_____
_____
_____

Action Steps

_____
_____
_____
_____
_____
_____
_____

WEEK OF _____ TO _____

Areas of my Life Wheel on my radar

_____

_____

_____

_____

MONDAY	TUESDAY	WEDNESDAY
5AM_____	5AM_____	5AM_____
_____	_____	_____
6AM_____	6AM_____	6AM_____
_____	_____	_____
7AM_____	7AM_____	7AM_____
_____	_____	_____
8AM_____	8AM_____	8AM_____
_____	_____	_____
9AM_____	9AM_____	9AM_____
_____	_____	_____
10AM_____	10AM_____	10AM_____
_____	_____	_____
11AM_____	11AM_____	11AM_____
_____	_____	_____
12PM_____	12PM_____	12PM_____
_____	_____	_____
1PM_____	1PM_____	1PM_____
_____	_____	_____
2PM_____	2PM_____	2PM_____
_____	_____	_____
3PM_____	3PM_____	3PM_____
_____	_____	_____
4PM_____	4PM_____	4PM_____
_____	_____	_____
5PM_____	5PM_____	5PM_____
_____	_____	_____
6PM_____	6PM_____	6PM_____
_____	_____	_____
7PM_____	7PM_____	7PM_____
_____	_____	_____
8PM_____	8PM_____	8PM_____
_____	_____	_____

SUNDAY

9AM_____

_____

10AM_____

_____

11AM_____

_____

12PM_____

_____

1PM_____

_____

2PM_____

_____

3PM_____

_____

4PM_____

_____

5PM_____

_____

6PM_____

_____

THURSDAY	FRIDAY	SATURDAY
5AM_____	5AM_____	9AM_____
6AM_____	6AM_____	10AM_____
7AM_____	7AM_____	11AM_____
8AM_____	8AM_____	12PM_____
9AM_____	9AM_____	1PM_____
10AM_____	10AM_____	2PM_____
11AM_____	11AM_____	3PM_____
12PM_____	12PM_____	4PM_____
1PM_____	1PM_____	5PM_____
2PM_____	2PM_____	6PM_____
3PM_____	3PM_____	
4PM_____	4PM_____	
5PM_____	5PM_____	
6PM_____	6PM_____	"I choose to attract what I value and want to experience." p. 105
7PM_____	7PM_____	
8PM_____	8PM_____	

Goals

_____
_____
_____
_____
_____
_____
_____

Action Steps

_____
_____
_____
_____
_____
_____

WEEK OF _____ TO _____

Areas of my Life Wheel on my radar

_____

_____

_____

_____

SUNDAY

9AM_____

_____

10AM_____

_____

11AM_____

_____

12PM_____

_____

1PM_____

_____

2PM_____

_____

3PM_____

_____

4PM_____

_____

5PM_____

_____

6PM_____

_____

MONDAY

5AM_____

_____

6AM_____

_____

7AM_____

_____

8AM_____

_____

9AM_____

_____

10AM_____

_____

11AM_____

_____

12PM_____

_____

1PM_____

_____

2PM_____

_____

3PM_____

_____

4PM_____

_____

5PM_____

_____

6PM_____

_____

7PM_____

_____

8PM_____

_____

TUESDAY

5AM_____

_____

6AM_____

_____

7AM_____

_____

8AM_____

_____

9AM_____

_____

10AM_____

_____

11AM_____

_____

12PM_____

_____

1PM_____

_____

2PM_____

_____

3PM_____

_____

4PM_____

_____

5PM_____

_____

6PM_____

_____

7PM_____

_____

8PM_____

_____

WEDNESDAY

5AM_____

_____

6AM_____

_____

7AM_____

_____

8AM_____

_____

9AM_____

_____

10AM_____

_____

11AM_____

_____

12PM_____

_____

1PM_____

_____

2PM_____

_____

3PM_____

_____

4PM_____

_____

5PM_____

_____

6PM_____

_____

7PM_____

_____

8PM_____

_____

THURSDAY	FRIDAY	SATURDAY
5AM_____	5AM_____	9AM_____
_____	_____	_____
6AM_____	6AM_____	10AM_____
_____	_____	_____
7AM_____	7AM_____	11AM_____
_____	_____	_____
8AM_____	8AM_____	12PM_____
_____	_____	_____
9AM_____	9AM_____	1PM_____
_____	_____	_____
10AM_____	10AM_____	2PM_____
_____	_____	_____
11AM_____	11AM_____	3PM_____
_____	_____	_____
12PM_____	12PM_____	4PM_____
_____	_____	_____
1PM_____	1PM_____	5PM_____
_____	_____	_____
2PM_____	2PM_____	6PM_____
_____	_____	_____
3PM_____	3PM_____	
_____	_____	
4PM_____	4PM_____	
_____	_____	
5PM_____	5PM_____	
_____	_____	"I choose to live
6PM_____	6PM_____	unlayered from the
_____	_____	inside out." p.105
7PM_____	7PM_____	
_____	_____	
8PM_____	8PM_____	
_____	_____	

Goals

_____
_____
_____
_____
_____
_____
_____

Action Steps

_____
_____
_____
_____
_____
_____
_____

WEEK OF _____ TO _____

	MONDAY	TUESDAY	WEDNESDAY

Areas of my Life Wheel on my radar

_____

_____

_____

_____

SUNDAY

9AM_____

_____

10AM_____

_____

11AM_____

_____

12PM_____

_____

1PM_____

_____

2PM_____

_____

3PM_____

_____

4PM_____

_____

5PM_____

_____

6PM_____

_____

MONDAY

5AM_____

_____

6AM_____

_____

7AM_____

_____

8AM_____

_____

9AM_____

_____

10AM_____

_____

11AM_____

_____

12PM_____

_____

1PM_____

_____

2PM_____

_____

3PM_____

_____

4PM_____

_____

5PM_____

_____

6PM_____

_____

7PM_____

_____

8PM_____

_____

TUESDAY

5AM_____

_____

6AM_____

_____

7AM_____

_____

8AM_____

_____

9AM_____

_____

10AM_____

_____

11AM_____

_____

12PM_____

_____

1PM_____

_____

2PM_____

_____

3PM_____

_____

4PM_____

_____

5PM_____

_____

6PM_____

_____

7PM_____

_____

8PM_____

_____

WEDNESDAY

5AM_____

_____

6AM_____

_____

7AM_____

_____

8AM_____

_____

9AM_____

_____

10AM_____

_____

11AM_____

_____

12PM_____

_____

1PM_____

_____

2PM_____

_____

3PM_____

_____

4PM_____

_____

5PM_____

_____

6PM_____

_____

7PM_____

_____

8PM_____

_____

THURSDAY	FRIDAY	SATURDAY
5AM_____	5AM_____	9AM_____
6AM_____	6AM_____	10AM_____
7AM_____	7AM_____	11AM_____
8AM_____	8AM_____	12PM_____
9AM_____	9AM_____	1PM_____
10AM_____	10AM_____	2PM_____
11AM_____	11AM_____	3PM_____
12PM_____	12PM_____	4PM_____
1PM_____	1PM_____	5PM_____
2PM_____	2PM_____	6PM_____
3PM_____	3PM_____	
4PM_____	4PM_____	
5PM_____	5PM_____	
6PM_____	6PM_____	"Unlocking more of your jail cells is dependent on the continued revelation of your layers." p.157
7PM_____	7PM_____	
8PM_____	8PM_____	

Goals

_____
_____
_____
_____
_____
_____
_____

Action Steps

_____
_____
_____
_____
_____
_____
_____

WEEK OF _____ TO _____

Areas of my Life Wheel on my radar

_____

_____

_____

_____

MONDAY	TUESDAY	WEDNESDAY
5AM_____	5AM_____	5AM_____
6AM_____	6AM_____	6AM_____
7AM_____	7AM_____	7AM_____
8AM_____	8AM_____	8AM_____
9AM_____	9AM_____	9AM_____
10AM_____	10AM_____	10AM_____
11AM_____	11AM_____	11AM_____
12PM_____	12PM_____	12PM_____
1PM_____	1PM_____	1PM_____
2PM_____	2PM_____	2PM_____
3PM_____	3PM_____	3PM_____
4PM_____	4PM_____	4PM_____
5PM_____	5PM_____	5PM_____
6PM_____	6PM_____	6PM_____
7PM_____	7PM_____	7PM_____
8PM_____	8PM_____	8PM_____

SUNDAY

9AM_____

10AM_____

11AM_____

12PM_____

1PM_____

2PM_____

3PM_____

4PM_____

5PM_____

6PM_____

THURSDAY	FRIDAY	SATURDAY
5AM_____	5AM_____	9AM_____
6AM_____	6AM_____	10AM_____
7AM_____	7AM_____	11AM_____
8AM_____	8AM_____	12PM_____
9AM_____	9AM_____	1PM_____
10AM_____	10AM_____	2PM_____
11AM_____	11AM_____	3PM_____
12PM_____	12PM_____	4PM_____
1PM_____	1PM_____	5PM_____
2PM_____	2PM_____	6PM_____
3PM_____	3PM_____	
4PM_____	4PM_____	
5PM_____	5PM_____	"I choose to look in the mirror and assess myself as needed." p.21
6PM_____	6PM_____	
7PM_____	7PM_____	
8PM_____	8PM_____	

Goals

_____
_____
_____
_____
_____
_____

Action Steps

_____
_____
_____
_____
_____
_____

NOTES_____

REJOICE!

Encourage yourself in your personal and professional life by taking advantage of opportunities to notice and celebrate accomplishments and milestones.

Successes

_____
_____
_____
_____
_____
_____
_____
_____

Completions

_____
_____
_____
_____
_____
_____
_____
_____

Special Events

_____
_____
_____
_____
_____
_____
_____
_____

Memories

_____
_____
_____
_____
_____
_____
_____
_____

MONTHLY SELF-REFLECTION:
Measuring the Net Value of Our Choices

What did you discover about yourself from the previous Life Wheel exercise? In what ways did that discovery surprise you? What specific awareness or revelations are most valuable to you?

_____
_____
_____
_____

Which area(s) did you focus on last month? Why?

_____
_____
_____
_____

How were your action steps effective or ineffective? What will you add, alter, or remove about those action steps going forward?

_____
_____
_____
_____

In what ways did having this awareness improve your personal life? Your professional life? The way you lead others?

_____
_____
_____
_____

Knowing we all fall short and have moments we don't achieve our goals and expectations, how will you extend grace to yourself to move forward?

_____
_____
_____
_____

Monthly Life Wheel Exercise

* Feel free to change or add an area. If it's important to you, it's important.

On a scale of one to ten, one being the lowest of the low and ten being best, rate your level of fulfillment in each category and record on the Life Wheel.

Business Calling _____   Financial Health _____

Physical Wellness _____   Relational Health _____

Intimacy _____   Personal Development _____

Play Time/Fun _____   Spiritual Wellness _____

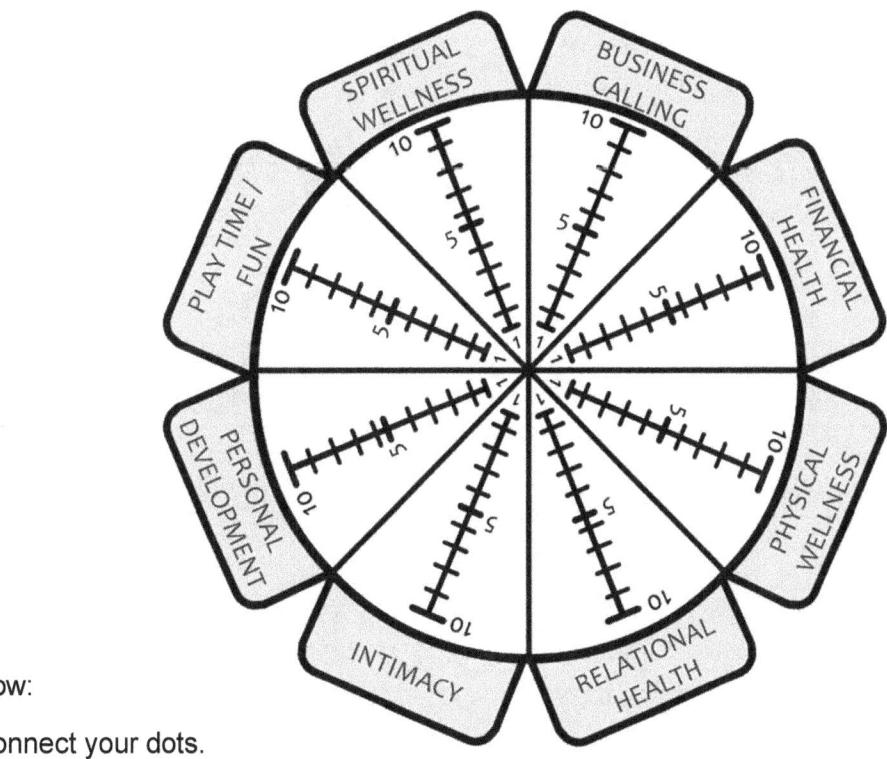

Now:

Connect your dots.

Determine what's on your radar.

What action steps can you take for improvement?

Record your action steps on your month overview. Reassess your steps each week and update accordingly using the central question: In this moment, what choice can I make and what action can I take to create the greatest net value?

Life Wheel Focus Area: *Playtime/Fun: External Perspective*
What about this area is important to me?
_____
_____

MONTH: _____   YEAR: _____

Action Steps
_____
_____
_____
_____
_____
_____
_____
_____
_____
_____
_____

OPPORTUNITIES
- ☐ _____
- ☐ _____
- ☐ _____
- ☐ _____
- ☐ _____
- ☐ _____
- ☐ _____
- ☐ _____
- ☐ _____
- ☐ _____

SUNDAY	MONDAY	TUESDAY

NOTES:

Focus Verse: "Restore to me the joy of your salvation and grant me a willing spirit, to sustain me." Psalms 51:12

How does this verse apply to my external world?

_____

WEDNESDAY	THURSDAY	FRIDAY	SATURDAY

"I choose to discover how my values influence my experiences." p. 105

WEEK OF _____ TO _____

Areas of my Life Wheel on my radar

_____

_____

_____

_____

SUNDAY

9AM_____

_____

10AM_____

_____

11AM_____

_____

12PM_____

_____

1PM_____

_____

2PM_____

_____

3PM_____

_____

4PM_____

_____

5PM_____

_____

6PM_____

_____

MONDAY

5AM_____

_____

6AM_____

_____

7AM_____

_____

8AM_____

_____

9AM_____

_____

10AM_____

_____

11AM_____

_____

12PM_____

_____

1PM_____

_____

2PM_____

_____

3PM_____

_____

4PM_____

_____

5PM_____

_____

6PM_____

_____

7PM_____

_____

8PM_____

_____

TUESDAY

5AM_____

_____

6AM_____

_____

7AM_____

_____

8AM_____

_____

9AM_____

_____

10AM_____

_____

11AM_____

_____

12PM_____

_____

1PM_____

_____

2PM_____

_____

3PM_____

_____

4PM_____

_____

5PM_____

_____

6PM_____

_____

7PM_____

_____

8PM_____

_____

WEDNESDAY

5AM_____

_____

6AM_____

_____

7AM_____

_____

8AM_____

_____

9AM_____

_____

10AM_____

_____

11AM_____

_____

12PM_____

_____

1PM_____

_____

2PM_____

_____

3PM_____

_____

4PM_____

_____

5PM_____

_____

6PM_____

_____

7PM_____

_____

8PM_____

_____

THURSDAY	FRIDAY	SATURDAY
5AM_____	5AM_____	9AM_____
6AM_____	6AM_____	10AM_____
7AM_____	7AM_____	11AM_____
8AM_____	8AM_____	12PM_____
9AM_____	9AM_____	1PM_____
10AM_____	10AM_____	2PM_____
11AM_____	11AM_____	3PM_____
12PM_____	12PM_____	4PM_____
1PM_____	1PM_____	5PM_____
2PM_____	2PM_____	6PM_____
3PM_____	3PM_____	
4PM_____	4PM_____	
5PM_____	5PM_____	"To be present from our core means being our authentic selves, living unlayered and from the inside out, and showing up fully present." p.130
6PM_____	6PM_____	
7PM_____	7PM_____	
8PM_____	8PM_____	

Goals

_____
_____
_____
_____
_____
_____
_____

Action Steps

_____
_____
_____
_____
_____
_____
_____

WEEK OF _____ TO _____

Areas of my Life Wheel on my radar

_____

_____

_____

_____

SUNDAY

9AM _____

_____

10AM _____

_____

11AM _____

_____

12PM _____

_____

1PM _____

_____

2PM _____

_____

3PM _____

_____

4PM _____

_____

5PM _____

_____

6PM _____

_____

MONDAY

5AM _____

_____

6AM _____

_____

7AM _____

_____

8AM _____

_____

9AM _____

_____

10AM _____

_____

11AM _____

_____

12PM _____

_____

1PM _____

_____

2PM _____

_____

3PM _____

_____

4PM _____

_____

5PM _____

_____

6PM _____

_____

7PM _____

_____

8PM _____

_____

TUESDAY

5AM _____

_____

6AM _____

_____

7AM _____

_____

8AM _____

_____

9AM _____

_____

10AM _____

_____

11AM _____

_____

12PM _____

_____

1PM _____

_____

2PM _____

_____

3PM _____

_____

4PM _____

_____

5PM _____

_____

6PM _____

_____

7PM _____

_____

8PM _____

_____

WEDNESDAY

5AM _____

_____

6AM _____

_____

7AM _____

_____

8AM _____

_____

9AM _____

_____

10AM _____

_____

11AM _____

_____

12PM _____

_____

1PM _____

_____

2PM _____

_____

3PM _____

_____

4PM _____

_____

5PM _____

_____

6PM _____

_____

7PM _____

_____

8PM _____

_____

THURSDAY	FRIDAY	SATURDAY
5AM_____	5AM_____	9AM_____
6AM_____	6AM_____	10AM_____
7AM_____	7AM_____	11AM_____
8AM_____	8AM_____	12PM_____
9AM_____	9AM_____	1PM_____
10AM_____	10AM_____	2PM_____
11AM_____	11AM_____	3PM_____
12PM_____	12PM_____	4PM_____
1PM_____	1PM_____	5PM_____
2PM_____	2PM_____	6PM_____
3PM_____	3PM_____	
4PM_____	4PM_____	
5PM_____	5PM_____	
6PM_____	6PM_____	
7PM_____	7PM_____	
8PM_____	8PM_____	

"Every experience we have gets labeled, organized, and filed depending on the filter we use when categorizing it. When we learn to change the filter and our perspective, we can change what would otherwise be crap into fertilizer."
p. 123

Goals

_____
_____
_____
_____
_____
_____
_____

Action Steps

_____
_____
_____
_____
_____
_____
_____

WEEK OF _____ TO _____

SUNDAY	MONDAY	TUESDAY	WEDNESDAY
	5AM_____	5AM_____	5AM_____
	6AM_____	6AM_____	6AM_____
	7AM_____	7AM_____	7AM_____
	8AM_____	8AM_____	8AM_____
9AM_____	9AM_____	9AM_____	9AM_____
10AM_____	10AM_____	10AM_____	10AM_____
11AM_____	11AM_____	11AM_____	11AM_____
12PM_____	12PM_____	12PM_____	12PM_____
1PM_____	1PM_____	1PM_____	1PM_____
2PM_____	2PM_____	2PM_____	2PM_____
3PM_____	3PM_____	3PM_____	3PM_____
4PM_____	4PM_____	4PM_____	4PM_____
5PM_____	5PM_____	5PM_____	5PM_____
6PM_____	6PM_____	6PM_____	6PM_____
	7PM_____	7PM_____	7PM_____
	8PM_____	8PM_____	8PM_____

THURSDAY	FRIDAY	SATURDAY
5AM_____	5AM_____	9AM_____
6AM_____	6AM_____	10AM_____
7AM_____	7AM_____	11AM_____
8AM_____	8AM_____	12PM_____
9AM_____	9AM_____	1PM_____
10AM_____	10AM_____	2PM_____
11AM_____	11AM_____	3PM_____
12PM_____	12PM_____	4PM_____
1PM_____	1PM_____	5PM_____
2PM_____	2PM_____	6PM_____
3PM_____	3PM_____	
4PM_____	4PM_____	
5PM_____	5PM_____	
6PM_____	6PM_____	
7PM_____	7PM_____	
8PM_____	8PM_____	

"We create potential pathways for relationships with others when we listen to them, then recognize and attempt to understand what they are bringing to the relationship, and how they connect with others." p.107

Goals

Action Steps

WEEK OF _____ TO _____

Areas of my Life Wheel on my radar

_____

_____

_____

_____

SUNDAY
9AM_____
_____
10AM_____
_____
11AM_____
_____
12PM_____
_____
1PM_____
_____
2PM_____
_____
3PM_____
_____
4PM_____
_____
5PM_____
_____
6PM_____
_____
_____

MONDAY	TUESDAY	WEDNESDAY
5AM_____	5AM_____	5AM_____
_____	_____	_____
6AM_____	6AM_____	6AM_____
_____	_____	_____
7AM_____	7AM_____	7AM_____
_____	_____	_____
8AM_____	8AM_____	8AM_____
_____	_____	_____
9AM_____	9AM_____	9AM_____
_____	_____	_____
10AM_____	10AM_____	10AM_____
_____	_____	_____
11AM_____	11AM_____	11AM_____
_____	_____	_____
12PM_____	12PM_____	12PM_____
_____	_____	_____
1PM_____	1PM_____	1PM_____
_____	_____	_____
2PM_____	2PM_____	2PM_____
_____	_____	_____
3PM_____	3PM_____	3PM_____
_____	_____	_____
4PM_____	4PM_____	4PM_____
_____	_____	_____
5PM_____	5PM_____	5PM_____
_____	_____	_____
6PM_____	6PM_____	6PM_____
_____	_____	_____
7PM_____	7PM_____	7PM_____
_____	_____	_____
8PM_____	8PM_____	8PM_____
_____	_____	_____

THURSDAY	FRIDAY	SATURDAY
5AM_____	5AM_____	9AM_____
6AM_____	6AM_____	10AM_____
7AM_____	7AM_____	11AM_____
8AM_____	8AM_____	12PM_____
9AM_____	9AM_____	1PM_____
10AM_____	10AM_____	2PM_____
11AM_____	11AM_____	3PM_____
12PM_____	12PM_____	4PM_____
1PM_____	1PM_____	5PM_____
2PM_____	2PM_____	6PM_____
3PM_____	3PM_____	
4PM_____	4PM_____	
5PM_____	5PM_____	"Even though we share a history with someone doesn't mean we've necessarily opened our layers to them." p. 114
6PM_____	6PM_____	
7PM_____	7PM_____	
8PM_____	8PM_____	

Goals

_____
_____
_____
_____
_____
_____
_____

Action Steps

_____
_____
_____
_____
_____
_____
_____

WEEK OF _____ TO _____

Areas of my Life
Wheel on my radar

_____

_____

_____

_____

SUNDAY

9AM_____
_____
10AM_____
_____
11AM_____
_____
12PM_____
_____
1PM_____
_____
2PM_____
_____
3PM_____
_____
4PM_____
_____
5PM_____
_____
6PM_____
_____

MONDAY

5AM_____
_____
6AM_____
_____
7AM_____
_____
8AM_____
_____
9AM_____
_____
10AM_____
_____
11AM_____
_____
12PM_____
_____
1PM_____
_____
2PM_____
_____
3PM_____
_____
4PM_____
_____
5PM_____
_____
6PM_____
_____
7PM_____
_____
8PM_____
_____

TUESDAY

5AM_____
_____
6AM_____
_____
7AM_____
_____
8AM_____
_____
9AM_____
_____
10AM_____
_____
11AM_____
_____
12PM_____
_____
1PM_____
_____
2PM_____
_____
3PM_____
_____
4PM_____
_____
5PM_____
_____
6PM_____
_____
7PM_____
_____
8PM_____
_____

WEDNESDAY

5AM_____
_____
6AM_____
_____
7AM_____
_____
8AM_____
_____
9AM_____
_____
10AM_____
_____
11AM_____
_____
12PM_____
_____
1PM_____
_____
2PM_____
_____
3PM_____
_____
4PM_____
_____
5PM_____
_____
6PM_____
_____
7PM_____
_____
8PM_____
_____

THURSDAY	FRIDAY	SATURDAY
5AM_____	5AM_____	9AM_____
6AM_____	6AM_____	10AM_____
7AM_____	7AM_____	11AM_____
8AM_____	8AM_____	12PM_____
9AM_____	9AM_____	1PM_____
10AM_____	10AM_____	2PM_____
11AM_____	11AM_____	3PM_____
12PM_____	12PM_____	4PM_____
1PM_____	1PM_____	5PM_____
2PM_____	2PM_____	6PM_____
3PM_____	3PM_____	
4PM_____	4PM_____	
5PM_____	5PM_____	
6PM_____	6PM_____	"I choose to see the results of my beliefs and my perceived purpose." p.144
7PM_____	7PM_____	
8PM_____	8PM_____	

Goals

_____
_____
_____
_____
_____
_____
_____

Action Steps

_____
_____
_____
_____
_____
_____

NOTES_____

NOTES

MONTHLY SELF-REFLECTION:
Measuring the Net Value of Our Choices

What did you discover about yourself from the previous Life Wheel exercise? In what ways did that discovery surprise you? What specific awareness or revelations are most valuable to you?

_____
_____
_____
_____

Which area(s) did you focus on last month? Why?

_____
_____
_____
_____

How were your action steps effective or ineffective? What will you add, alter, or remove about those action steps going forward?

_____
_____
_____
_____

In what ways did having this awareness improve your personal life? Your professional life? The way you lead others?

_____
_____
_____
_____

Knowing we all fall short and have moments we don't achieve our goals and expectations, how will you extend grace to yourself to move forward?

_____
_____
_____
_____

Monthly Life Wheel Exercise

* Feel free to change or add an area. If it's important to you, it's important.

On a scale of one to ten, one being the lowest of the low and ten being best, rate your level of fulfillment in each category and record on the Life Wheel.

Business Calling _____   Financial Health _____

Physical Wellness _____   Relational Health _____

Intimacy _____   Personal Development _____

Play Time/Fun _____   Spiritual Wellness _____

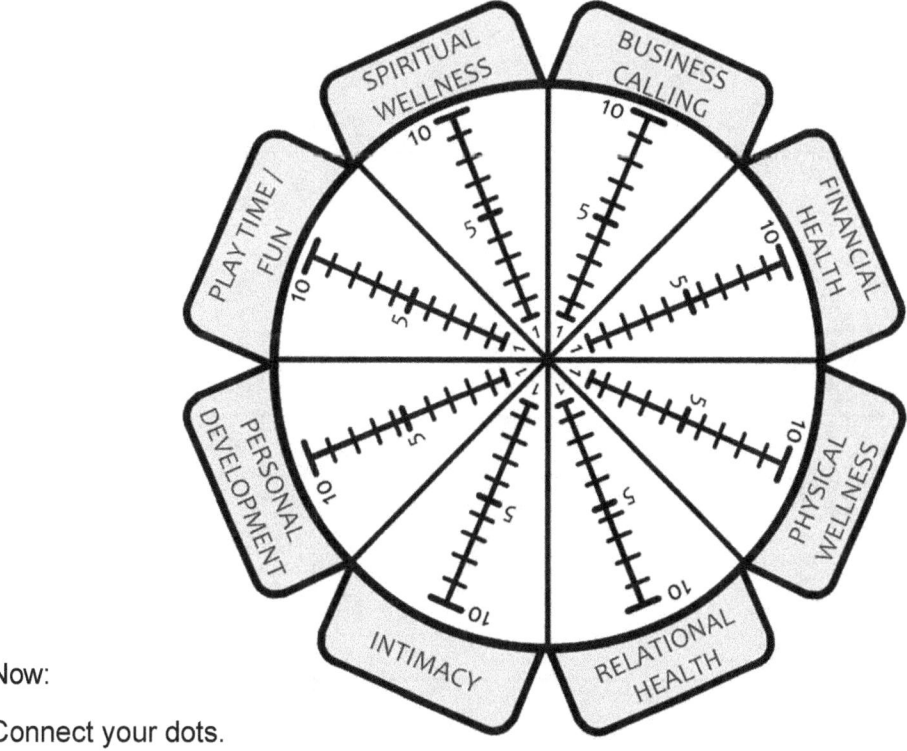

Now:

Connect your dots.

Determine what's on your radar.

What action steps can you take for improvement?

Record your action steps on your month overview. Reassess your steps each week and update accordingly using the central question: In this moment, what choice can I make and what action can I take to create the greatest net value?

Life Wheel Focus Area: *Playtime/Fun: Internal Perspective*
What about this area is important to me?

_____

_____

MONTH: _____   YEAR: _____

Action Steps

_____
_____
_____
_____
_____
_____
_____
_____
_____
_____

OPPORTUNITIES

- ☐ _____
- ☐ _____
- ☐ _____
- ☐ _____
- ☐ _____
- ☐ _____
- ☐ _____
- ☐ _____
- ☐ _____
- ☐ _____

SUNDAY	MONDAY	TUESDAY

NOTES:

Focus Verse: "Ask the Lord your God for a sign, whether in the deepest depths or in the highest heights." Isaiah 7:11

How does this verse apply to my internal world?

_____

WEDNESDAY	THURSDAY	FRIDAY	SATURDAY

"I choose to learn and understand how my heart, soul, and mind connect in my inner labyrinth." p. 144

Areas of my Life Wheel on my radar

_____

_____

_____

_____

SUNDAY	MONDAY	TUESDAY	WEDNESDAY
	5AM_____	5AM_____	5AM_____
9AM_____	6AM_____	6AM_____	6AM_____
10AM_____	7AM_____	7AM_____	7AM_____
11AM_____	8AM_____	8AM_____	8AM_____
12PM_____	9AM_____	9AM_____	9AM_____
1PM_____	10AM_____	10AM_____	10AM_____
2PM_____	11AM_____	11AM_____	11AM_____
3PM_____	12PM_____	12PM_____	12PM_____
4PM_____	1PM_____	1PM_____	1PM_____
5PM_____	2PM_____	2PM_____	2PM_____
6PM_____	3PM_____	3PM_____	3PM_____
	4PM_____	4PM_____	4PM_____
	5PM_____	5PM_____	5PM_____
	6PM_____	6PM_____	6PM_____
	7PM_____	7PM_____	7PM_____
	8PM_____	8PM_____	8PM_____

THURSDAY	FRIDAY	SATURDAY
5AM_____	5AM_____	9AM_____
6AM_____	6AM_____	10AM_____
7AM_____	7AM_____	11AM_____
8AM_____	8AM_____	12PM_____
9AM_____	9AM_____	1PM_____
10AM_____	10AM_____	2PM_____
11AM_____	11AM_____	3PM_____
12PM_____	12PM_____	4PM_____
1PM_____	1PM_____	5PM_____
2PM_____	2PM_____	6PM_____
3PM_____	3PM_____	
4PM_____	4PM_____	
5PM_____	5PM_____	"I choose to listen and validate the ideas of others." p. 133
6PM_____	6PM_____	
7PM_____	7PM_____	
8PM_____	8PM_____	

Goals

_____
_____
_____
_____
_____
_____
_____

Action Steps

_____
_____
_____
_____
_____
_____
_____

Areas of my Life Wheel on my radar

_____

_____

_____

_____

SUNDAY

9AM_____

10AM_____

11AM_____

12PM_____

1PM_____

2PM_____

3PM_____

4PM_____

5PM_____

6PM_____

MONDAY

5AM_____

6AM_____

7AM_____

8AM_____

9AM_____

10AM_____

11AM_____

12PM_____

1PM_____

2PM_____

3PM_____

4PM_____

5PM_____

6PM_____

7PM_____

8PM_____

TUESDAY

5AM_____

6AM_____

7AM_____

8AM_____

9AM_____

10AM_____

11AM_____

12PM_____

1PM_____

2PM_____

3PM_____

4PM_____

5PM_____

6PM_____

7PM_____

8PM_____

WEDNESDAY

5AM_____

6AM_____

7AM_____

8AM_____

9AM_____

10AM_____

11AM_____

12PM_____

1PM_____

2PM_____

3PM_____

4PM_____

5PM_____

6PM_____

7PM_____

8PM_____

THURSDAY	FRIDAY	SATURDAY
5AM_____	5AM_____	9AM_____
_____	_____	_____
6AM_____	6AM_____	10AM_____
_____	_____	_____
7AM_____	7AM_____	11AM_____
_____	_____	_____
8AM_____	8AM_____	12PM_____
_____	_____	_____
9AM_____	9AM_____	1PM_____
_____	_____	_____
10AM_____	10AM_____	2PM_____
_____	_____	_____
11AM_____	11AM_____	3PM_____
_____	_____	_____
12PM_____	12PM_____	4PM_____
_____	_____	_____
1PM_____	1PM_____	5PM_____
_____	_____	_____
2PM_____	2PM_____	6PM_____
_____	_____	_____
3PM_____	3PM_____	
_____	_____	
4PM_____	4PM_____	
_____	_____	
5PM_____	5PM_____	
_____	_____	"I choose to get to
6PM_____	6PM_____	the bottom of every
_____	_____	*why* in my life." p.41
7PM_____	7PM_____	
_____	_____	
8PM_____	8PM_____	
_____	_____	

Goals

_____
_____
_____
_____
_____
_____

Action Steps

_____
_____
_____
_____
_____
_____

WEEK OF _____ TO _____

Areas of my Life Wheel on my radar

_____

_____

_____

_____

SUNDAY

9AM_____

_____

10AM_____

_____

11AM_____

_____

12PM_____

_____

1PM_____

_____

2PM_____

_____

3PM_____

_____

4PM_____

_____

5PM_____

_____

6PM_____

_____

MONDAY

5AM_____

_____

6AM_____

_____

7AM_____

_____

8AM_____

_____

9AM_____

_____

10AM_____

_____

11AM_____

_____

12PM_____

_____

1PM_____

_____

2PM_____

_____

3PM_____

_____

4PM_____

_____

5PM_____

_____

6PM_____

_____

7PM_____

_____

8PM_____

_____

TUESDAY

5AM_____

_____

6AM_____

_____

7AM_____

_____

8AM_____

_____

9AM_____

_____

10AM_____

_____

11AM_____

_____

12PM_____

_____

1PM_____

_____

2PM_____

_____

3PM_____

_____

4PM_____

_____

5PM_____

_____

6PM_____

_____

7PM_____

_____

8PM_____

_____

WEDNESDAY

5AM_____

_____

6AM_____

_____

7AM_____

_____

8AM_____

_____

9AM_____

_____

10AM_____

_____

11AM_____

_____

12PM_____

_____

1PM_____

_____

2PM_____

_____

3PM_____

_____

4PM_____

_____

5PM_____

_____

6PM_____

_____

7PM_____

_____

8PM_____

_____

THURSDAY	FRIDAY	SATURDAY
5AM_____	5AM_____	9AM_____
6AM_____	6AM_____	10AM_____
7AM_____	7AM_____	11AM_____
8AM_____	8AM_____	12PM_____
9AM_____	9AM_____	1PM_____
10AM_____	10AM_____	2PM_____
11AM_____	11AM_____	3PM_____
12PM_____	12PM_____	4PM_____
1PM_____	1PM_____	5PM_____
2PM_____	2PM_____	6PM_____
3PM_____	3PM_____	
4PM_____	4PM_____	
5PM_____	5PM_____	
6PM_____	6PM_____	"I choose to initiate authentic connections by living from my core self." p. 133
7PM_____	7PM_____	
8PM_____	8PM_____	

Goals

_____
_____
_____
_____
_____
_____
_____

Action Steps

_____
_____
_____
_____
_____
_____
_____

WEEK OF _____ TO _____

Areas of my Life
Wheel on my radar

_____

_____

_____

_____

SUNDAY	MONDAY	TUESDAY	WEDNESDAY
9AM_____	5AM_____	5AM_____	5AM_____
_____	_____	_____	_____
10AM_____	6AM_____	6AM_____	6AM_____
_____	_____	_____	_____
11AM_____	7AM_____	7AM_____	7AM_____
_____	_____	_____	_____
12PM_____	8AM_____	8AM_____	8AM_____
_____	_____	_____	_____
1PM_____	9AM_____	9AM_____	9AM_____
_____	_____	_____	_____
2PM_____	10AM_____	10AM_____	10AM_____
_____	_____	_____	_____
3PM_____	11AM_____	11AM_____	11AM_____
_____	_____	_____	_____
4PM_____	12PM_____	12PM_____	12PM_____
_____	_____	_____	_____
5PM_____	1PM_____	1PM_____	1PM_____
_____	_____	_____	_____
6PM_____	2PM_____	2PM_____	2PM_____
_____	_____	_____	_____
	3PM_____	3PM_____	3PM_____
	_____	_____	_____
	4PM_____	4PM_____	4PM_____
	_____	_____	_____
	5PM_____	5PM_____	5PM_____
	_____	_____	_____
	6PM_____	6PM_____	6PM_____
	_____	_____	_____
	7PM_____	7PM_____	7PM_____
	_____	_____	_____
	8PM_____	8PM_____	8PM_____
	_____	_____	_____

THURSDAY	FRIDAY	SATURDAY
5AM_____	5AM_____	9AM_____
_____	_____	_____
6AM_____	6AM_____	10AM_____
_____	_____	_____
7AM_____	7AM_____	11AM_____
_____	_____	_____
8AM_____	8AM_____	12PM_____
_____	_____	_____
9AM_____	9AM_____	1PM_____
_____	_____	_____
10AM_____	10AM_____	2PM_____
_____	_____	_____
11AM_____	11AM_____	3PM_____
_____	_____	_____
12PM_____	12PM_____	4PM_____
_____	_____	_____
1PM_____	1PM_____	5PM_____
_____	_____	_____
2PM_____	2PM_____	6PM_____
_____	_____	_____
3PM_____	3PM_____	
_____	_____	
4PM_____	4PM_____	
_____	_____	
5PM_____	5PM_____	"Choosing to be silent and observe, or be silent and listen, or even be silent and learn is very difficult for many." p. 138
_____	_____	
6PM_____	6PM_____	
_____	_____	
7PM_____	7PM_____	
_____	_____	
8PM_____	8PM_____	
_____	_____	
_____	_____	

Goals

_____
_____
_____
_____
_____
_____
_____

Action Steps

_____
_____
_____
_____
_____
_____
_____

WEEK OF _____ TO _____

MONDAY	TUESDAY	WEDNESDAY
5AM_____	5AM_____	5AM_____
6AM_____	6AM_____	6AM_____
7AM_____	7AM_____	7AM_____
8AM_____	8AM_____	8AM_____
9AM_____	9AM_____	9AM_____
10AM_____	10AM_____	10AM_____
11AM_____	11AM_____	11AM_____
12PM_____	12PM_____	12PM_____
1PM_____	1PM_____	1PM_____
2PM_____	2PM_____	2PM_____
3PM_____	3PM_____	3PM_____
4PM_____	4PM_____	4PM_____
5PM_____	5PM_____	5PM_____
6PM_____	6PM_____	6PM_____
7PM_____	7PM_____	7PM_____
8PM_____	8PM_____	8PM_____

SUNDAY

9AM_____

10AM_____

11AM_____

12PM_____

1PM_____

2PM_____

3PM_____

4PM_____

5PM_____

6PM_____

THURSDAY	FRIDAY	SATURDAY	Goals
5AM_____	5AM_____	9AM_____	_____
_____	_____	_____	_____
6AM_____	6AM_____	10AM_____	_____
_____	_____	_____	_____
7AM_____	7AM_____	11AM_____	_____
_____	_____	_____	_____
8AM_____	8AM_____	12PM_____	_____
_____	_____	_____	_____
9AM_____	9AM_____	1PM_____	_____
_____	_____	_____	
10AM_____	10AM_____	2PM_____	
_____	_____	_____	
11AM_____	11AM_____	3PM_____	
_____	_____	_____	
12PM_____	12PM_____	4PM_____	
_____	_____	_____	
1PM_____	1PM_____	5PM_____	
_____	_____	_____	
2PM_____	2PM_____	6PM_____	Action Steps
_____	_____	_____	
3PM_____	3PM_____		
_____	_____		_____
4PM_____	4PM_____		_____
_____	_____		_____
5PM_____	5PM_____	"I choose to reassess my Life Wheel and the actions I take to increase my life satisfaction. " p.144	_____
_____	_____		_____
6PM_____	6PM_____		_____
_____	_____		_____
7PM_____	7PM_____		_____
_____	_____		_____
8PM_____	8PM_____		_____
_____	_____		

NOTES_____
_____
_____
_____
_____
_____
_____
_____
_____
_____
_____
_____
_____
_____
_____
_____
_____
_____
_____
_____
_____
_____
_____
_____
_____
_____
_____
_____
_____
_____
_____
_____
_____
_____
_____
_____
_____
_____
_____

NOTES_____

MONTHLY SELF-REFLECTION:
Measuring the Net Value of Our Choices

What did you discover about yourself from the previous Life Wheel exercise? In what ways did that discovery surprise you? What specific awareness or revelations are most valuable to you?

_____
_____
_____
_____

Which area(s) did you focus on last month? Why?

_____
_____
_____
_____

How were your action steps effective or ineffective? What will you add, alter, or remove about those action steps going forward?

_____
_____
_____
_____

In what ways did having this awareness improve your personal life? Your professional life? The way you lead others?

_____
_____
_____
_____

Knowing we all fall short and have moments we don't achieve our goals and expectations, how will you extend grace to yourself to move forward?

_____
_____
_____
_____

Monthly Life Wheel Exercise

* Feel free to change or add an area. If it's important to you, it's important.

On a scale of one to ten, one being the lowest of the low and ten being best, rate your level of fulfillment in each category and record on the Life Wheel.

Business Calling _____   Financial Health _____

Physical Wellness _____   Relational Health _____

Intimacy _____   Personal Development _____

Play Time/Fun _____   Spiritual Wellness _____

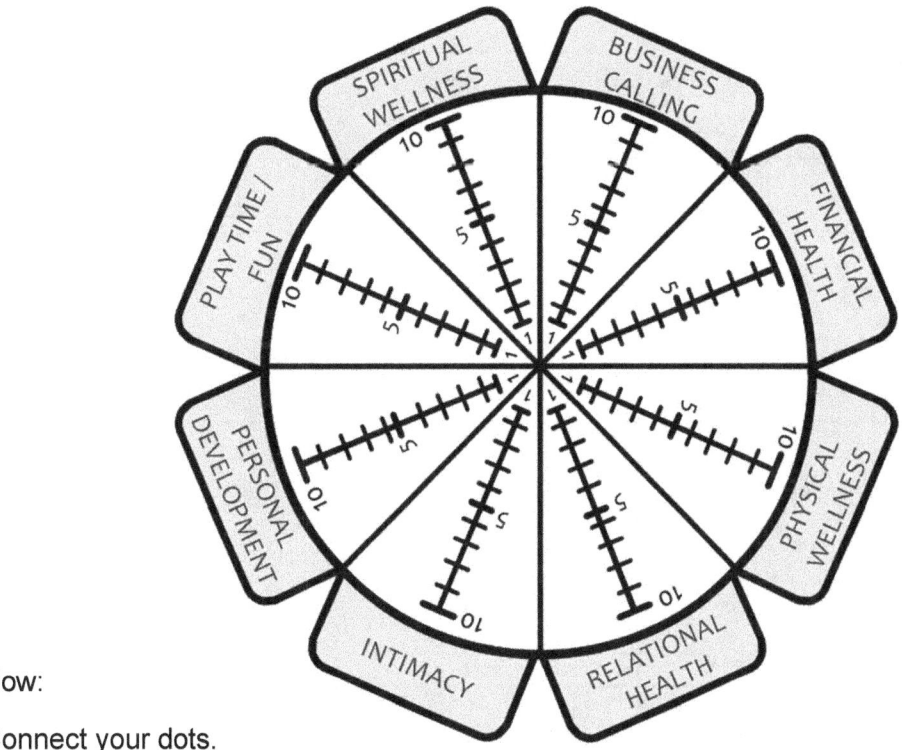

Now:

Connect your dots.

Determine what's on your radar.

What action steps can you take for improvement?

Record your action steps on your month overview. Reassess your steps each week and update accordingly using the central question: In this moment, what choice can I make and what action can I take to create the greatest net value?

Life Wheel Focus Area: *Spiritual Wellness: External Perspective*

What about this area is important to me?

_____

_____

MONTH: _____   YEAR: _____

Action Steps

_____

_____

_____

_____

_____

_____

_____

_____

_____

_____

_____

OPPORTUNITIES

- ☐ _____
- ☐ _____
- ☐ _____
- ☐ _____
- ☐ _____
- ☐ _____
- ☐ _____
- ☐ _____
- ☐ _____
- ☐ _____

SUNDAY	MONDAY	TUESDAY

NOTES:

Focus Verse: "Therefore, my brothers and sisters, make every effort to confirm your calling and election. For if you do these things, you will never stumble," 2 Peter 1:10

How does this verse apply to my external world?

_____

WEDNESDAY	THURSDAY	FRIDAY	SATURDAY

"When we learn to value each other from a place of grace, we can build connections that give each other permission to cross the relational bridge at a depth not many people earn." p. 131

WEEK OF _____ TO _____

Areas of my Life Wheel on my radar

_____

_____

_____

_____

SUNDAY

9AM_____

_____

10AM_____

_____

11AM_____

_____

12PM_____

_____

1PM_____

_____

2PM_____

_____

3PM_____

_____

4PM_____

_____

5PM_____

_____

6PM_____

_____

MONDAY

5AM_____

_____

6AM_____

_____

7AM_____

_____

8AM_____

_____

9AM_____

_____

10AM_____

_____

11AM_____

_____

12PM_____

_____

1PM_____

_____

2PM_____

_____

3PM_____

_____

4PM_____

_____

5PM_____

_____

6PM_____

_____

7PM_____

_____

8PM_____

_____

TUESDAY

5AM_____

_____

6AM_____

_____

7AM_____

_____

8AM_____

_____

9AM_____

_____

10AM_____

_____

11AM_____

_____

12PM_____

_____

1PM_____

_____

2PM_____

_____

3PM_____

_____

4PM_____

_____

5PM_____

_____

6PM_____

_____

7PM_____

_____

8PM_____

_____

WEDNESDAY

5AM_____

_____

6AM_____

_____

7AM_____

_____

8AM_____

_____

9AM_____

_____

10AM_____

_____

11AM_____

_____

12PM_____

_____

1PM_____

_____

2PM_____

_____

3PM_____

_____

4PM_____

_____

5PM_____

_____

6PM_____

_____

7PM_____

_____

8PM_____

_____

THURSDAY	FRIDAY	SATURDAY
5AM_____	5AM_____	9AM_____
_____	_____	_____
6AM_____	6AM_____	10AM_____
_____	_____	_____
7AM_____	7AM_____	11AM_____
_____	_____	_____
8AM_____	8AM_____	12PM_____
_____	_____	_____
9AM_____	9AM_____	1PM_____
_____	_____	_____
10AM_____	10AM_____	2PM_____
_____	_____	_____
11AM_____	11AM_____	3PM_____
_____	_____	_____
12PM_____	12PM_____	4PM_____
_____	_____	_____
1PM_____	1PM_____	5PM_____
_____	_____	_____
2PM_____	2PM_____	6PM_____
_____	_____	_____
3PM_____	3PM_____	
_____	_____	
4PM_____	4PM_____	
_____	_____	
5PM_____	5PM_____	
_____	_____	
6PM_____	6PM_____	"Analyzing these bridges within ourselves will help us recognize a concern or obstacle that surfaces inside us when interacting with others." p. 111
_____	_____	
7PM_____	7PM_____	
_____	_____	
8PM_____	8PM_____	
_____	_____	

Goals

_____
_____
_____
_____
_____
_____
_____

Action Steps

_____
_____
_____
_____
_____
_____
_____

WEEK OF _____ TO _____

Areas of my Life Wheel on my radar

_____

_____

_____

_____

SUNDAY

9AM_____

10AM_____

11AM_____

12PM_____

1PM_____

2PM_____

3PM_____

4PM_____

5PM_____

6PM_____

MONDAY

5AM_____

6AM_____

7AM_____

8AM_____

9AM_____

10AM_____

11AM_____

12PM_____

1PM_____

2PM_____

3PM_____

4PM_____

5PM_____

6PM_____

7PM_____

8PM_____

TUESDAY

5AM_____

6AM_____

7AM_____

8AM_____

9AM_____

10AM_____

11AM_____

12PM_____

1PM_____

2PM_____

3PM_____

4PM_____

5PM_____

6PM_____

7PM_____

8PM_____

WEDNESDAY

5AM_____

6AM_____

7AM_____

8AM_____

9AM_____

10AM_____

11AM_____

12PM_____

1PM_____

2PM_____

3PM_____

4PM_____

5PM_____

6PM_____

7PM_____

8PM_____

THURSDAY	FRIDAY	SATURDAY
5AM_____	5AM_____	9AM_____
6AM_____	6AM_____	10AM_____
7AM_____	7AM_____	11AM_____
8AM_____	8AM_____	12PM_____
9AM_____	9AM_____	1PM_____
10AM_____	10AM_____	2PM_____
11AM_____	11AM_____	3PM_____
12PM_____	12PM_____	4PM_____
1PM_____	1PM_____	5PM_____
2PM_____	2PM_____	6PM_____
3PM_____	3PM_____	
4PM_____	4PM_____	
5PM_____	5PM_____	
6PM_____	6PM_____	"Every morning you wake up presents a gift, on opportunity." p. 91
7PM_____	7PM_____	
8PM_____	8PM_____	

Goals

_____
_____
_____
_____
_____
_____
_____

Action Steps

_____
_____
_____
_____
_____
_____
_____

WEEK OF _____ TO _____

Areas of my Life Wheel on my radar

_____

_____

_____

_____

SUNDAY

9AM_____
_____
10AM_____
_____
11AM_____
_____
12PM_____
_____
1PM_____
_____
2PM_____
_____
3PM_____
_____
4PM_____
_____
5PM_____
_____
6PM_____
_____

MONDAY

5AM_____
_____
6AM_____
_____
7AM_____
_____
8AM_____
_____
9AM_____
_____
10AM_____
_____
11AM_____
_____
12PM_____
_____
1PM_____
_____
2PM_____
_____
3PM_____
_____
4PM_____
_____
5PM_____
_____
6PM_____
_____
7PM_____
_____
8PM_____
_____

TUESDAY

5AM_____
_____
6AM_____
_____
7AM_____
_____
8AM_____
_____
9AM_____
_____
10AM_____
_____
11AM_____
_____
12PM_____
_____
1PM_____
_____
2PM_____
_____
3PM_____
_____
4PM_____
_____
5PM_____
_____
6PM_____
_____
7PM_____
_____
8PM_____
_____

WEDNESDAY

5AM_____
_____
6AM_____
_____
7AM_____
_____
8AM_____
_____
9AM_____
_____
10AM_____
_____
11AM_____
_____
12PM_____
_____
1PM_____
_____
2PM_____
_____
3PM_____
_____
4PM_____
_____
5PM_____
_____
6PM_____
_____
7PM_____
_____
8PM_____
_____

THURSDAY	FRIDAY	SATURDAY
5AM_____	5AM_____	9AM_____
_____	_____	_____
6AM_____	6AM_____	10AM_____
_____	_____	_____
7AM_____	7AM_____	11AM_____
_____	_____	_____
8AM_____	8AM_____	12PM_____
_____	_____	_____
9AM_____	9AM_____	1PM_____
_____	_____	_____
10AM_____	10AM_____	2PM_____
_____	_____	_____
11AM_____	11AM_____	3PM_____
_____	_____	_____
12PM_____	12PM_____	4PM_____
_____	_____	_____
1PM_____	1PM_____	5PM_____
_____	_____	_____
2PM_____	2PM_____	6PM_____
_____	_____	_____
3PM_____	3PM_____	_____
_____	_____	
4PM_____	4PM_____	
_____	_____	
5PM_____	5PM_____	
_____	_____	"I choose to meet each person where they are." p. 133
6PM_____	6PM_____	
_____	_____	
7PM_____	7PM_____	
_____	_____	
8PM_____	8PM_____	
_____	_____	

Goals

_____
_____
_____
_____
_____
_____
_____

Action Steps

_____
_____
_____
_____
_____
_____
_____

WEEK OF _____ TO _____

Areas of my Life Wheel on my radar

_____

_____

_____

_____

MONDAY	TUESDAY	WEDNESDAY
5AM _____	5AM _____	5AM _____
6AM _____	6AM _____	6AM _____
7AM _____	7AM _____	7AM _____
8AM _____	8AM _____	8AM _____
9AM _____	9AM _____	9AM _____
10AM _____	10AM _____	10AM _____
11AM _____	11AM _____	11AM _____
12PM _____	12PM _____	12PM _____
1PM _____	1PM _____	1PM _____
2PM _____	2PM _____	2PM _____
3PM _____	3PM _____	3PM _____
4PM _____	4PM _____	4PM _____
5PM _____	5PM _____	5PM _____
6PM _____	6PM _____	6PM _____
7PM _____	7PM _____	7PM _____
8PM _____	8PM _____	8PM _____

SUNDAY

9AM _____

10AM _____

11AM _____

12PM _____

1PM _____

2PM _____

3PM _____

4PM _____

5PM _____

6PM _____

THURSDAY	FRIDAY	SATURDAY
5AM_____	5AM_____	9AM_____
6AM_____	6AM_____	10AM_____
7AM_____	7AM_____	11AM_____
8AM_____	8AM_____	12PM_____
9AM_____	9AM_____	1PM_____
10AM_____	10AM_____	2PM_____
11AM_____	11AM_____	3PM_____
12PM_____	12PM_____	4PM_____
1PM_____	1PM_____	5PM_____
2PM_____	2PM_____	6PM_____
3PM_____	3PM_____	
4PM_____	4PM_____	
5PM_____	5PM_____	
6PM_____	6PM_____	"True freedom is exactly that – living without walls and without feeling a need for them."
7PM_____	7PM_____	p. 52
8PM_____	8PM_____	

Goals

_____
_____
_____
_____
_____
_____
_____

Action Steps

_____
_____
_____
_____
_____
_____
_____

Areas of my Life Wheel on my radar

_____

_____

_____

_____

SUNDAY

9AM_____

_____

10AM_____

_____

11AM_____

_____

12PM_____

_____

1PM_____

_____

2PM_____

_____

3PM_____

_____

4PM_____

_____

5PM_____

_____

6PM_____

_____

MONDAY

5AM_____

_____

6AM_____

_____

7AM_____

_____

8AM_____

_____

9AM_____

_____

10AM_____

_____

11AM_____

_____

12PM_____

_____

1PM_____

_____

2PM_____

_____

3PM_____

_____

4PM_____

_____

5PM_____

_____

6PM_____

_____

7PM_____

_____

8PM_____

_____

TUESDAY

5AM_____

_____

6AM_____

_____

7AM_____

_____

8AM_____

_____

9AM_____

_____

10AM_____

_____

11AM_____

_____

12PM_____

_____

1PM_____

_____

2PM_____

_____

3PM_____

_____

4PM_____

_____

5PM_____

_____

6PM_____

_____

7PM_____

_____

8PM_____

_____

WEDNESDAY

5AM_____

_____

6AM_____

_____

7AM_____

_____

8AM_____

_____

9AM_____

_____

10AM_____

_____

11AM_____

_____

12PM_____

_____

1PM_____

_____

2PM_____

_____

3PM_____

_____

4PM_____

_____

5PM_____

_____

6PM_____

_____

7PM_____

_____

8PM_____

_____

THURSDAY	FRIDAY	SATURDAY
5AM_____	5AM_____	9AM_____
6AM_____	6AM_____	10AM_____
7AM_____	7AM_____	11AM_____
8AM_____	8AM_____	12PM_____
9AM_____	9AM_____	1PM_____
10AM_____	10AM_____	2PM_____
11AM_____	11AM_____	3PM_____
12PM_____	12PM_____	4PM_____
1PM_____	1PM_____	5PM_____
2PM_____	2PM_____	6PM_____
3PM_____	3PM_____	
4PM_____	4PM_____	
5PM_____	5PM_____	
6PM_____	6PM_____	"I am one of many Onion Slayers." p. 21
7PM_____	7PM_____	
8PM_____	8PM_____	

Goals

_____
_____
_____
_____
_____
_____
_____

Action Steps

_____
_____
_____
_____
_____
_____
_____

NOTES_____

NOTES_____

MONTHLY SELF-REFLECTION:
Measuring the Net Value of Our Choices

What did you discover about yourself from the previous Life Wheel exercise? In what ways did that discovery surprise you? What specific awareness or revelations are most valuable to you?

_____

_____

_____

_____

Which area(s) did you focus on last month? Why?

_____

_____

_____

_____

How were your action steps effective or ineffective? What will you add, alter, or remove about those action steps going forward?

_____

_____

_____

_____

In what ways did having this awareness improve your personal life? Your professional life? The way you lead others?

_____

_____

_____

_____

Knowing we all fall short and have moments we don't achieve our goals and expectations, how will you extend grace to yourself to move forward?

_____

_____

_____

_____

Monthly Life Wheel Exercise

* Feel free to change or add an area. If it's important to you, it's important.

On a scale of one to ten, one being the lowest of the low and ten being best, rate your level of fulfillment in each category and record on the Life Wheel.

Business Calling _____   Financial Health _____

Physical Wellness _____   Relational Health _____

Intimacy _____   Personal Development _____

Play Time/Fun _____   Spiritual Wellness _____

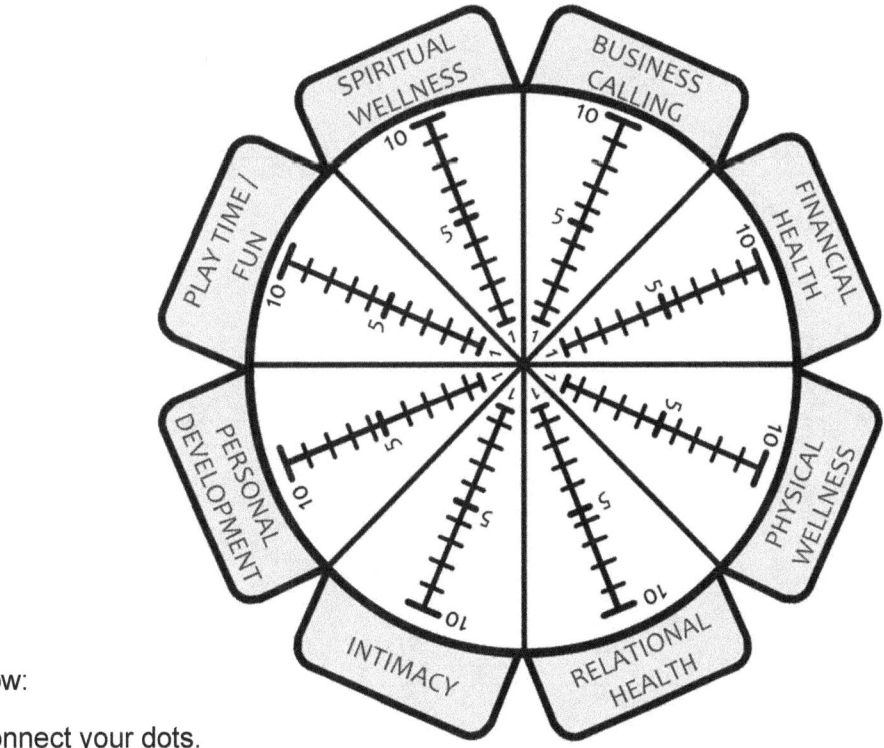

Now:

Connect your dots.

Determine what's on your radar.

What action steps can you take for improvement?

Record your action steps on your month overview. Reassess your steps each week and update accordingly using the central question: In this moment, what choice can I make and what action can I take to create the greatest net value?

Life Wheel Focus Area: *Spiritual Wellness: Internal Perspective*
What about this area is important to me?

_____

_____

MONTH: _____   YEAR: _____

Action Steps

_____

_____

_____

_____

_____

_____

_____

_____

_____

_____

_____

_____

OPPORTUNITIES

- [ ] _____
- [ ] _____
- [ ] _____
- [ ] _____
- [ ] _____
- [ ] _____
- [ ] _____
- [ ] _____
- [ ] _____
- [ ] _____

SUNDAY	MONDAY	TUESDAY

NOTES:

Focus Verse: "He heals the brokenhearted and binds up their wounds."
Psalm 147:3

How does this verse apply to my internal world?

_____

WEDNESDAY	THURSDAY	FRIDAY	SATURDAY

"We must embrace being our own leader, whether or not we are directly responsible for others in our personal or professional life." p.33-34

WEEK OF _____ TO _____

Areas of my Life
Wheel on my radar

_____

_____

_____

_____

SUNDAY
9AM_____
_____
10AM_____
_____
11AM_____
_____
12PM_____
_____
1PM_____
_____
2PM_____
_____
3PM_____
_____
4PM_____
_____
5PM_____
_____
6PM_____
_____

MONDAY	TUESDAY	WEDNESDAY
5AM_____	5AM_____	5AM_____
_____	_____	_____
6AM_____	6AM_____	6AM_____
_____	_____	_____
7AM_____	7AM_____	7AM_____
_____	_____	_____
8AM_____	8AM_____	8AM_____
_____	_____	_____
9AM_____	9AM_____	9AM_____
_____	_____	_____
10AM_____	10AM_____	10AM_____
_____	_____	_____
11AM_____	11AM_____	11AM_____
_____	_____	_____
12PM_____	12PM_____	12PM_____
_____	_____	_____
1PM_____	1PM_____	1PM_____
_____	_____	_____
2PM_____	2PM_____	2PM_____
_____	_____	_____
3PM_____	3PM_____	3PM_____
_____	_____	_____
4PM_____	4PM_____	4PM_____
_____	_____	_____
5PM_____	5PM_____	5PM_____
_____	_____	_____
6PM_____	6PM_____	6PM_____
_____	_____	_____
7PM_____	7PM_____	7PM_____
_____	_____	_____
8PM_____	8PM_____	8PM_____
_____	_____	_____

THURSDAY	FRIDAY	SATURDAY
5AM_____	5AM_____	9AM_____
6AM_____	6AM_____	10AM_____
7AM_____	7AM_____	11AM_____
8AM_____	8AM_____	12PM_____
9AM_____	9AM_____	1PM_____
10AM_____	10AM_____	2PM_____
11AM_____	11AM_____	3PM_____
12PM_____	12PM_____	4PM_____
1PM_____	1PM_____	5PM_____
2PM_____	2PM_____	6PM_____
3PM_____	3PM_____	
4PM_____	4PM_____	
5PM_____	5PM_____	"As walking through a physical labyrinth is much more than a simple walk through a garden, navigating our inner labyrinth is more than a mental, emotional, and singularly spiritual process." p. 137
6PM_____	6PM_____	
7PM_____	7PM_____	
8PM_____	8PM_____	

Goals

_____
_____
_____
_____
_____
_____
_____
_____

Action Steps

_____
_____
_____
_____
_____
_____
_____
_____

WEEK OF _____ TO _____

Areas of my Life Wheel on my radar

_____

_____

_____

_____

MONDAY

5AM_____
_____
6AM_____
_____
7AM_____
_____
8AM_____
_____
9AM_____
_____
10AM_____
_____
11AM_____
_____
12PM_____
_____
1PM_____
_____
2PM_____
_____
3PM_____
_____
4PM_____
_____
5PM_____
_____
6PM_____
_____
7PM_____
_____
8PM_____
_____

TUESDAY

5AM_____
_____
6AM_____
_____
7AM_____
_____
8AM_____
_____
9AM_____
_____
10AM_____
_____
11AM_____
_____
12PM_____
_____
1PM_____
_____
2PM_____
_____
3PM_____
_____
4PM_____
_____
5PM_____
_____
6PM_____
_____
7PM_____
_____
8PM_____
_____

WEDNESDAY

5AM_____
_____
6AM_____
_____
7AM_____
_____
8AM_____
_____
9AM_____
_____
10AM_____
_____
11AM_____
_____
12PM_____
_____
1PM_____
_____
2PM_____
_____
3PM_____
_____
4PM_____
_____
5PM_____
_____
6PM_____
_____
7PM_____
_____
8PM_____
_____

SUNDAY

9AM_____
_____
10AM_____
_____
11AM_____
_____
12PM_____
_____
1PM_____
_____
2PM_____
_____
3PM_____
_____
4PM_____
_____
5PM_____
_____
6PM_____
_____

THURSDAY	FRIDAY	SATURDAY
5AM_____	5AM_____	9AM_____
6AM_____	6AM_____	10AM_____
7AM_____	7AM_____	11AM_____
8AM_____	8AM_____	12PM_____
9AM_____	9AM_____	1PM_____
10AM_____	10AM_____	2PM_____
11AM_____	11AM_____	3PM_____
12PM_____	12PM_____	4PM_____
1PM_____	1PM_____	5PM_____
2PM_____	2PM_____	6PM_____
3PM_____	3PM_____	
4PM_____	4PM_____	
5PM_____	5PM_____	"I choose to gently and kindly ask questions to discover where the other person is on the bridge." p. 133
6PM_____	6PM_____	
7PM_____	7PM_____	
8PM_____	8PM_____	

Goals

_____
_____
_____
_____
_____
_____
_____

Action Steps

_____
_____
_____
_____
_____
_____
_____

WEEK OF _____ TO _____

Areas of my Life
Wheel on my radar

_____

_____

_____

_____

SUNDAY

9AM_____

_____

10AM_____

_____

11AM_____

_____

12PM_____

_____

1PM_____

_____

2PM_____

_____

3PM_____

_____

4PM_____

_____

5PM_____

_____

6PM_____

_____

MONDAY

5AM_____

_____

6AM_____

_____

7AM_____

_____

8AM_____

_____

9AM_____

_____

10AM_____

_____

11AM_____

_____

12PM_____

_____

1PM_____

_____

2PM_____

_____

3PM_____

_____

4PM_____

_____

5PM_____

_____

6PM_____

_____

7PM_____

_____

8PM_____

_____

TUESDAY

5AM_____

_____

6AM_____

_____

7AM_____

_____

8AM_____

_____

9AM_____

_____

10AM_____

_____

11AM_____

_____

12PM_____

_____

1PM_____

_____

2PM_____

_____

3PM_____

_____

4PM_____

_____

5PM_____

_____

6PM_____

_____

7PM_____

_____

8PM_____

_____

WEDNESDAY

5AM_____

_____

6AM_____

_____

7AM_____

_____

8AM_____

_____

9AM_____

_____

10AM_____

_____

11AM_____

_____

12PM_____

_____

1PM_____

_____

2PM_____

_____

3PM_____

_____

4PM_____

_____

5PM_____

_____

6PM_____

_____

7PM_____

_____

8PM_____

_____

THURSDAY	FRIDAY	SATURDAY	Goals
5AM_____	5AM_____	9AM_____	
_____	_____	_____	_____
6AM_____	6AM_____	10AM_____	_____
_____	_____	_____	_____
7AM_____	7AM_____	11AM_____	_____
_____	_____	_____	_____
8AM_____	8AM_____	12PM_____	_____
_____	_____	_____	_____
9AM_____	9AM_____	1PM_____	_____
_____	_____	_____	_____
10AM_____	10AM_____	2PM_____	_____
_____	_____	_____	
11AM_____	11AM_____	3PM_____	
_____	_____	_____	
12PM_____	12PM_____	4PM_____	
_____	_____	_____	
1PM_____	1PM_____	5PM_____	
_____	_____	_____	
2PM_____	2PM_____	6PM_____	Action Steps
_____	_____	_____	
3PM_____	3PM_____		
_____	_____		_____
4PM_____	4PM_____		_____
_____	_____		_____
5PM_____	5PM_____		_____
_____	_____		_____
6PM_____	6PM_____	"I choose to navigate my inner labyrinth." p. 144	_____
_____	_____		_____
7PM_____	7PM_____		_____
_____	_____		_____
8PM_____	8PM_____		_____
_____	_____		_____

WEEK OF _____ TO _____

Areas of my Life
Wheel on my radar

_____

_____

_____

_____

SUNDAY

9AM_____

_____

10AM_____

_____

11AM_____

_____

12PM_____

_____

1PM_____

_____

2PM_____

_____

3PM_____

_____

4PM_____

_____

5PM_____

_____

6PM_____

_____

MONDAY

5AM_____

_____

6AM_____

_____

7AM_____

_____

8AM_____

_____

9AM_____

_____

10AM_____

_____

11AM_____

_____

12PM_____

_____

1PM_____

_____

2PM_____

_____

3PM_____

_____

4PM_____

_____

5PM_____

_____

6PM_____

_____

7PM_____

_____

8PM_____

_____

TUESDAY

5AM_____

_____

6AM_____

_____

7AM_____

_____

8AM_____

_____

9AM_____

_____

10AM_____

_____

11AM_____

_____

12PM_____

_____

1PM_____

_____

2PM_____

_____

3PM_____

_____

4PM_____

_____

5PM_____

_____

6PM_____

_____

7PM_____

_____

8PM_____

_____

WEDNESDAY

5AM_____

_____

6AM_____

_____

7AM_____

_____

8AM_____

_____

9AM_____

_____

10AM_____

_____

11AM_____

_____

12PM_____

_____

1PM_____

_____

2PM_____

_____

3PM_____

_____

4PM_____

_____

5PM_____

_____

6PM_____

_____

7PM_____

_____

8PM_____

_____

THURSDAY	FRIDAY	SATURDAY
5AM_____	5AM_____	9AM_____
_____	_____	_____
6AM_____	6AM_____	10AM_____
_____	_____	_____
7AM_____	7AM_____	11AM_____
_____	_____	_____
8AM_____	8AM_____	12PM_____
_____	_____	_____
9AM_____	9AM_____	1PM_____
_____	_____	_____
10AM_____	10AM_____	2PM_____
_____	_____	_____
11AM_____	11AM_____	3PM_____
_____	_____	_____
12PM_____	12PM_____	4PM_____
_____	_____	_____
1PM_____	1PM_____	5PM_____
_____	_____	_____
2PM_____	2PM_____	6PM_____
_____	_____	_____
3PM_____	3PM_____	
_____	_____	
4PM_____	4PM_____	
_____	_____	
5PM_____	5PM_____	
_____	_____	
6PM_____	6PM_____	"I choose to walk deeper into my own layers." p. 144
_____	_____	
7PM_____	7PM_____	
_____	_____	
8PM_____	8PM_____	
_____	_____	

Goals

_____
_____
_____
_____
_____
_____
_____

Action Steps

_____
_____
_____
_____
_____
_____
_____

WEEK OF _____ TO _____

Areas of my Life Wheel on my radar

_____

_____

_____

_____

SUNDAY

9AM_____

_____

10AM_____

_____

11AM_____

_____

12PM_____

_____

1PM_____

_____

2PM_____

_____

3PM_____

_____

4PM_____

_____

5PM_____

_____

6PM_____

_____

MONDAY

5AM_____

_____

6AM_____

_____

7AM_____

_____

8AM_____

_____

9AM_____

_____

10AM_____

_____

11AM_____

_____

12PM_____

_____

1PM_____

_____

2PM_____

_____

3PM_____

_____

4PM_____

_____

5PM_____

_____

6PM_____

_____

7PM_____

_____

8PM_____

_____

TUESDAY

5AM_____

_____

6AM_____

_____

7AM_____

_____

8AM_____

_____

9AM_____

_____

10AM_____

_____

11AM_____

_____

12PM_____

_____

1PM_____

_____

2PM_____

_____

3PM_____

_____

4PM_____

_____

5PM_____

_____

6PM_____

_____

7PM_____

_____

8PM_____

_____

WEDNESDAY

5AM_____

_____

6AM_____

_____

7AM_____

_____

8AM_____

_____

9AM_____

_____

10AM_____

_____

11AM_____

_____

12PM_____

_____

1PM_____

_____

2PM_____

_____

3PM_____

_____

4PM_____

_____

5PM_____

_____

6PM_____

_____

7PM_____

_____

8PM_____

_____

THURSDAY	FRIDAY	SATURDAY	Goals
5AM _____	5AM _____	9AM _____	
6AM _____	6AM _____	10AM _____	_____
7AM _____	7AM _____	11AM _____	_____
8AM _____	8AM _____	12PM _____	_____
9AM _____	9AM _____	1PM _____	_____
10AM _____	10AM _____	2PM _____	_____
11AM _____	11AM _____	3PM _____	_____
12PM _____	12PM _____	4PM _____	
1PM _____	1PM _____	5PM _____	
2PM _____	2PM _____	6PM _____	Action Steps
3PM _____	3PM _____		_____
4PM _____	4PM _____		_____
5PM _____	5PM _____	"Unveil the layers of your story to reveal your highest potential."	_____
6PM _____	6PM _____		_____
7PM _____	7PM _____		_____
8PM _____	8PM _____		_____

NOTES

REJOICE!

Encourage yourself in your personal and professional life by taking advantage of opportunities to notice and celebrate accomplishments and milestones.

Successes

_____

_____

_____

_____

_____

_____

_____

Completions

_____

_____

_____

_____

_____

_____

_____

Special Events

_____

_____

_____

_____

_____

_____

_____

Memories

_____

_____

_____

_____

_____

_____

_____

MONTHLY SELF-REFLECTION:
Measuring the Net Value of Our Choices

What did you discover about yourself from the previous Life Wheel exercise? In what ways did that discovery surprise you? What specific awareness or revelations are most valuable to you?

_____
_____
_____
_____

Which area(s) did you focus on last month? Why?

_____
_____
_____
_____

How were your action steps effective or ineffective? What will you add, alter, or remove about those action steps going forward?

_____
_____
_____
_____

In what ways did having this awareness improve your personal life? Your professional life? The way you lead others?

_____
_____
_____
_____

Knowing we all fall short and have moments we don't achieve our goals and expectations, how will you extend grace to yourself to move forward?

_____
_____
_____
_____

NOTES